CLASS AND CLASS STRUCTURE

Edited with an Introduction

by

ALAN HUNT

LAWRENCE AND WISHART
LONDON

Lawrence and Wishart Ltd
39 Museum Street
London WC1

First published 1977
Copyright © Lawrence and Wishart, 1977

ISBN 85315 402 3

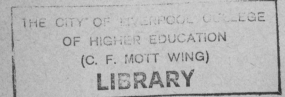
Printed in Great Britain by
The Camelot Press Ltd, Southampton

CONTENTS

INTRODUCTION

The essays collected in this book were presented at a conference organised by the Sociology Group of the Communist Party of Great Britain, held in November 1976 at the Polytechnic of the South Bank in London. The scope and purpose of this introduction is limited to placing the discussions and debates in their general context, and to introducing the individual papers. I will avoid the temptation to enter into the debates and controversies themselves because my own position is stated in my paper.

The unifying feature of contemporary Marxism is its common reaction against the version of Marxism that has dominated the communist and workers movement for a number of decades. This 'traditional' or 'orthodox' Marxism can be identified by the labels of reductionism and economism. Reductionism involves a version of historical materialism which presents all social phenomena as 'reducible' to, or explicable in terms of, the 'economic base'. Thus political struggles or social ideologies are explained as manifestations or 'reflections' of economic forces. In this presentation Marxism is reduced to a set of relatively simple and universal 'laws'.

The following essays, despite their differences of approach, stand on common ground in their rejection of reductionism. The error of reductionism is that it leads to the conclusion that, in analysing political or social events, these can be 'read off' from an analysis of economic developments, which in turn implies that we have only to analyse the economic development of capitalism in order to be able to explain all the social and political phenomena of its contemporary form. This interpretation of Marxism necessarily involves an assumption that the economy has secreted within it the essential constituents of *all* social developments. Such a position is guilty of 'essentialism', that is of seeing the 'economy' as embodying the essence of all social phenomenon which are then simply expressed or made manifest in the social world.

It is this tradition which modern Marxism has confronted. In doing

so it has re-examined the major texts by Marx himself, many more of
which have become available, often for the first time, to a wider
audience. At the same time the work of Marxists who had, in an earlier
period, challenged dogmatic Marxism was taken up again and played
an important part in recent discussions; this is particularly true of the
work of Georg Lukács and Antonio Gramsci.

In challenging a simplistic and mechanical interpretation of Marx,
contemporary Marxism has needed to question many of the taken-for-
granted concepts and theories, and to re-examine the very basis of
Marxist theory. Much of this work has consciously elevated the
importance of *theory* which had lain dormant for so long during the
Stalin era. One of the consequences of this attention to theoretical issues
has been that the work produced has been not only difficult, but often
very abstract and not of any apparent direct political significance. Even
Louis Althusser, who has played such a central role in recent Marxist
discussion, has in his self-criticism pointed to a tendency towards
theoreticism in his own work.[*1]

One brief comment is perhaps necessary with reference to the place
of theory. While Marxists have always correctly placed emphasis upon
the integration of theory and practice, dogmatic Marxism has tended to
seek to reduce this integration to a simple or direct relation in which
theory has to subserve practice. Thus, every theoretical position was
judged by its apparent political implications (this was carried over into
every field of culture and science). But theory and practice can never
exist in a simple or direct relation: one cannot be simply deduced or
translated into the other. It is not surprising that the resurgence of a
strengthened Marxist theory should sometimes be difficult or even
inaccessible; this is a small price to pay for the existence of the viable and
healthy discussion that is now taking place *within* Marxism.

The concepts 'class', 'class structure' and 'class struggle' occupy a
central place within Marxist theory. Not only are they of theoretical
importance but they are also of powerful political significance. The
analysis of class and class structure is of central importance in any
Marxist analysis of a specific historical or contemporary situation –
that is, of any specific conjuncture. It is on the basis of such analysis
that the groundwork is laid on which the political strategies of
revolutionary and socialist movements are developed, not in the sense

* See reference notes at end of each chapter.

that the strategy can be deduced from the class analysis but rather that it provides the context within which the political strategy can be generated.

While the central focus of these essays is upon the question of class, the majority of them have a wider focus within which important differences emerge. If we are to reject the interpretation of Marxism in which all social phenomena can be 'reduced to' or derived from the economic, then the immediate question arises: what is the nature of the relationship between the economic, on the one hand, and the political and ideological on the other? This question lies at the heart of the current debate within Marxism. The essays in this book embody a range of different approaches. For example, Stuart Hall develops his analysis within terms of the solution posed, in particular by Engels in his famous 'late letters',[2] which rests on the idea of the 'relative autonomy' of politics and ideology. Nicos Poulantzas, on the other hand, operates with a position that derives from Althusser in which the relative autonomy, or 'the determination in the last instance by the economic', derives from the dual role of the economic level, as a distinct level within the social totality, alongside political and ideological levels, which at the same time provide the structure which determines the causal effects of the distinct levels. Both of these positions are criticised by Paul Hirst who argues that neither of them provides a theoretically coherent solution; in their place he posits the very controversial thesis that there is a 'necessary non-correspondence between the economic and the political'.

Stuart Hall's opening paper provides an extensive discussion of Marx's own analysis of class. For Marx the identification of classes, that is the distribution of individuals or agents to specific classes by reference to their relationship to the productive process, was not a major problem. His central concern was with the relational character of classes, in particular the opposition *between* classes, as providing the distinctive character of classes themselves. Stuart Hall traces Marx's analysis of class from its early formulations in *The Communist Manifesto* through to the later treatment in *Capital* and the historical texts, *The Eighteenth Brumaire of Louis Bonaparte* and *The Civil War in France*. He sees in Marx a transition from a relatively simple dichotomy between bourgeoisie and proletariat (or between lords and serfs, or slave-owners and slaves), when a direct relationship is posited between contending economic classes in which the political class struggle is the reflex or result of their polar opposition, to the 'complex simplification' of Marx's later works, where, without abandoning the concept of fundamental dichotomy, Marx no longer treats politics as the direct expression of class interests, but posits contending political *forces* (and not classes as such) as engaging in struggle. This requires an analysis, which Marx himself never fully or systematically developed, of 'the specificity of the political' or of the 'relative autonomy' of the political struggle. Finally Stuart Hall argues that we should not counterpose an 'early' and a 'late' Marx but grasp the fundamental unity of his approach, which is one that requires continuing creative work to grapple with the problems of the complexity of this unity.

The next three essays all have as their primary focus the initially narrower problem of the identification of the working class and its boundaries.

Vic Allen insists that the modern working class is necessarily more extensive and more complex in its internal relations than the working class of early industrial capitalism. We are therefore required to examine the problem of the differentiation of the contemporary working class if we are to be able to analyse its politics and consciousness. He argues that we can identify distinct 'labour markets' through which different sections of wage-labourers sell their labour power, and that different positions within such markets embody different forms and levels of skills and differential power relations with respect to the employers. The different labour markets are not simply economically defined; they are also ideologically constituted. The important implication that flows from this analysis is that it makes it possible to understand the particular contradictions and antagonisms that can and *do* exist amongst and between wage-labourers, and consequently facilitates the analysis of the different levels and forms of class struggle and class consciousness within the working class. This type of analysis also points towards a tendency within advanced capitalism for the emergence of common responses from wider sections of wage-labourers, epitomised by the growth of trade union organisation amongst non-manual workers.

My own paper on the identification of the working class directly takes issue with the analysis advanced by Poulantzas in *Classes in Contemporary Capitalism*.[3] I set out to explore the political and strategic implications of the alternatives of a 'broad' as against a 'narrow' definition of the working class. The paper rejects Poulantzas's attempt to restrict the working class to productive labourers (labour which produces surplus value), since this fails to reveal any fundamental division or cleavage that separates productive and non-productive workers. My argument also rejects the designation of all non-productive workers as members of a new class, the 'new petty bourgeoisie'. I take issue with his method of attributing ideological and political positions to non-productive workers, from which he derives a convergence of class position between the 'new' and the 'traditional' petty bourgeoisie. I seek to develop an alternative solution which bases itself upon Marx's concept of 'social relations of production' which needs to be seen as embodying a number of different levels. In particular I suggest it is necessary to distinguish between immediate and class relations of production. The implication leads to the proposition that the 'economic' level specifies the potential boundary or parameter of the working class (as sellers of labour power/non-owners of the means of production), while 'class relations' embody political and ideological determinants which allow us to distinguish between the class practices adopted by particular sections or fractions of the working class.

The presence of Nicos Poulantzas at the conference ensured that his recent work was a major focus of attention. He spoke as a member of the Greek Communist Party (Interior) and insisted that his work should be seen as an intervention in the strategic debates of the European communist and socialist movements. His contribution took the form of a response to the papers that had been given. He had not been able to read them in advance and his intervention therefore took a polemical form which has been preserved in his essay. Only a minimum of changes have been made in effecting the transition from his spoken intervention to its printed form.

Poulantzas concentrated his attention on the theses which he advanced in *Classes in Contemporary Capitalism*. He argued that the conception of the working class as being composed of all wage-labourers is fundamentally social-democratic. Wages are the form of distribution within the capitalist mode of production. The basis of Marxist analysis of class must therefore found itself, he claimed, on the process of the creation of surplus-value; and it is for this reason that the distinction between productive and non-productive labour is essential in determining the boundary of the working class. The analysis in terms of the creation of surplus-value establishes the negative proposition that non-productive employees are *not* part of the working class. The positive identification of their class membership is provided by the political and ideological elements, in particular with reference to their authority and control within the labour process and the significance of mental labour. These criteria establish their class location as a 'new petty bourgeoisie'.

The political implications that stem from his theoretical position are spelt out. If salaried workers are members of another class, then in developing a strategy of class alliance between the working class and the new petty bourgeoisie we must take account of their *specific* class interests, and must not assume that they necessarily share the same general interests as the working class. Further it allows us to explore the processes through which certain sections of the salaried employees are polarised towards the working class. The analysis of the new petty bourgeoisie makes possible a developed view of the essential conditions for constituting the hegemony of the working class in the transition to socialism.

Paul Hirst argues that in attempting to escape from reductionism Poulantzas ends up by advancing an unacceptable, albeit complicated, economism. Despite his attempt to deny it, Poulantzas ends up by equating economic classes and political forces. Hirst proceeds to develop a critique of the notion of 'relative autonomy' and the 'structural causality' which lies at the heart of the positions of both Poulantzas and Althusser. 'Relative autonomy' is an untenable position because it tries to have the best of both worlds, on the one hand to retain some notion of the ultimate correspondence between the economic and the political, on the other, to assert the specificity of politics and political class struggle. The central problem facing Marxist theory, according to Hirst, is that it has to make a choice between economism/reductionism (whether in a simple or complex variant) and recognising the 'necessary non-correspondence' between political forces and economic classes. This position requires us to recognise that classes as such do not directly fight out the class struggle, but rather that it is political forces which cannot be analysed as 'representing' classes, which are the agents which engage in struggle. Such a position, he argues, requires Marxists to engage in concrete analysis of particular political situations; only in

INTRODUCTION 13

this way is it possible to arrive at appropriate political strategies for socialist transformation.

Jean Gardiner sets out to overcome another distortion that arises from a narrow economistic analysis. Traditional Marxist analysis has had relatively little to say about the position of women in the class structure; and this analysis cannot be advanced simply by designating women into classes by reference to the males upon whom they are economically dependent. The position of women in capitalist society is determined by the dual operation of the class division *and* the sexual division of labour. The analysis of the sexual division of labour makes it possible to understand the present context in which an increasing percentage of women are entering the labour-market while, at the same time, they are increasingly dependent upon marriage and their role within the family. This dimension helps in analysing the specific role of women in the labour process and their distribution within the workforce. Jean Gardiner concludes by arguing that an analysis of the impact of the sexual division of labour is necessary if we are to grapple with the questions which must confront the trade union and socialist movement with respect to the relationship between women and the organised class struggle.

John Westergaard approaches the analysis of class by a less direct route. He sets out to examine the recent theory of 'corporatism' which has not only achieved academic expression but has also been taken up by *The Times*. The corporatist theory argues that Britain is rapidly moving towards a new form of society, the corporate society or mode of production, which is neither capitalist nor socialist. State economic intervention is presented as abolishing the market determination of wages, prices and profit and, though private legal ownership is retained, and even the capitalist market system itself. Westergaard asks: can we accept that the corporate economy is no longer capitalist? His answer is strongly in the negative, since the corporate economy retains the same basic inequality of distribution which is the essence of the class division of capitalism. 'Inequality' is identified as the primary characteristic of class society; it is the structure of inequality which determines the class structure of society. This emphasis on inequality is seen as representing a very different line of analysis to that embodied in the other essays, most of which would regard inequality as being a result or consequence of class division but not its fundamental or determining characteristic. Westergaard argues that his approach is more in keeping with the humanist tradition within Marxism.

The essays presented here engage in the major theoretical and political issues within the Marxist analysis of classes and of class structure. At the same time the discussion of class provides a framework for the exploration of some of the more general issues in Marxist theory and politics.

REFERENCES

1. Louis Althusser, *Essays in Self-Criticism*, New Left Books, London, 1976.
2. Engels to Bloch, Schmidt, Mehring and Starkenburg (Borgius), *Marx–Engels Selected Correspondence*, pp. 394, 396, 433 and 441, Moscow, 1975.
3. New Left Books, London, 1975.

THE 'POLITICAL' AND THE 'ECONOMIC' IN MARX'S THEORY OF CLASSES

Stuart Hall

The limits on this paper will be immediately obvious. It is not possible, here, to present anything like a comprehensive or systematic 'survey' of Marx's theory of classes. First, classes, class relations and class struggle are concepts central to everything which Marx wrote – including, of course, the major work of *Capital* on the 'laws of motion' of the capitalist mode of production, where the discussion of classes is postponed to the very end, and was in fact tantalisingly incomplete. A comprehensive account of 'Marx on class' would thus amount to a reconstruction of his entire work. Second, there is no such homogeneous entity or object as a 'theory of class', in the singular, to be exposited. Marx wrote about class and class struggle at each of the major moments of his work. As we know, these texts have different degrees of status and purposes – a matter which crucially affects the level, the aspect, the degree of abstraction, etc., through which the question is approached. The polemic against the Left Hegelians in *The German Ideology*, the organisational purpose and rhetorical simplifications of *The Communist Manifesto*, the conjunctural political analyses of *The Class Struggles in France*, the theoretical labour of *The Grundrisse* and *Capital* – each, because of the difference in its aim and address, *inflects* the problem of classes differently.

We know from his comments and correspondence – for example, concerning the differences in the manner of exposition as between the 'working notebooks' of the *Grundrisse* and *Capital* – that Marx took this question of mode of presentation very seriously. For example, in his letter of 1 February 1859, he writes to Weydemeyer about the intended order of publication of the first four sections of Book I of *Capital*: 'You understand the *political* reasons which have moved me to hold back the third Chapter on "Capital" until I have established myself again . . .'

(*MESC*, p. 105). Third, we know that these different texts are also to some degree bound and governed by the problematics within which Marx was thinking and writing at the time. These changed and altered as Marx's thinking developed. Althusser is correct in his argument that Marx's 'discoveries' are in some critical sense bound up with the 'breaks' between one problematic and another. Without necessarily accepting the severe and finalist manner in which Althusser has 'periodised' Marx's work, with the aid of the powerful instrument of the 'epistemological rupture' – an operation from which, in any case, Althusser has subsequently taken his necessary distance (cf. the major 'revisions' in Althusser, 1976) – his intervention *does* prevent us from ever reading Marx again in such a way as to constitute, by a prospective-retrospective sleight-of-hand, a single, homogeneous 'Marxism', always on its preordained way, from the *1844 Manuscripts* to the *Civil War in France*, towards its given, teleological end. It prevents as 'essentialist', and therefore closed, reading of Marx such as would suggest that all that is really discovered in *Capital* is already 'present', in embryo, in the *1844 Manuscripts* – that all the texts can be taken together, as a linear progression, and read transparently for their inevitable tendency, for what they incipiently lead to. Such a reading not only does an injustice to Marx, it also establishes a false and misleading picture of how theoretical work has to be done, and obscures the retreats and detours by which it advances and develops. It incites in us a 'lazy' Marxism, suggesting that there is no critical work left for us to do in really grappling with the differences and the developments in Marx's own work – and that all we have to do is rest on the 'obviousness' of the 'Marxism' always latent in Marx's texts. This kind of Marxist 'common sense' has done profound damage to Marxism as a living and developing practice – including the necessary practice of struggle *in* theory itself. Such a linear transparency in Marx must be constantly and vigorously challenged.

In part, what is involved, then, is a particular practice of reading – one which tries to hold together the logic of the argument and exposition of a text, within the matrix of propositions and concepts which makes its discourse possible, which generates it. In the limited passages and texts discussed in this paper, much depends on the project to develop a mode of theoretical work of this kind. It involves ceasing to take a text at its face value, as a closed object. This applies both where the text is resoundingly 'obvious', and where it is obviously complex, even obscure. The question of the class struggle is manifestly *present* in every line and paragraph of *The Communist Manifesto*. Yet the concept of classes which generates that text is, as we hope to show, not immediately graspable from its luminous surface. *Capital* is precisely the reverse – a complex, theoretical text, which has centrally as its object the capitalist mode of production; and which appears, for long stretches to have 'postponed' the class struggle to another level, another moment. One of the most difficult exercises is to 'read' the *Manifesto* for the concept of the relation between classes and modes of production which lies at its heart; and to 'read' the laws and motion of capital in *Capital* in terms of the class struggle. In the latter instance, Marx gives us a beautiful insight – again, in a letter he wrote to Engels (30 April 1868) – into how the two relate. He is resuming the argument, essentially, of *Capital* III. He goes over some of the most complex – and technical – of concepts: the constitution of an 'average rate of profit'; the relation between the different branches of production; the problem of the transformation 'of value into price of production'; the tendency of the rate of profit to fall. Then he returns, at the end, to what constitutes the 'starting point for the vulgar economist': the famous Trinitarian Formula (the dismantling of which, *in extenso*, in *Capital* III is one of the richest and most devastating theoretical passages of that work). This is the 'formula' which appeared to 'explain' the distribution of profit in terms of the harmonious return of each proportionate part to its appointed factor in capitalist production: 'rent originating from the land, profit (interest) from capital, wages from labour'. In revealing the 'real' movement behind this distribution, he has dismantled its 'apparent form'; but this is no mere 'theoretical' demystification. 'Finally, since these three (wages, rent, profit (interest) constitute the respective sources of income of the three classes of landowners, capitalists and wage labourers, we have, in conclusion the *class struggle* into which the movement and the analysis of the whole business [*Scheisse*, shit, in the original] resolves itself' (*MESC*, 1975).

Althusser has given us a protocol for 'reading' theoretical texts in this way – the method of a 'symptomatic reading'. My own remarks above stop some way short of proposing the full 'symptomatic reading' of Marx's work. The idea has its source, of course, in Freud's theory of the formation of 'symptoms' in the discourse of the patient, in his important

work on the *Interpretation of Dreams*. The difficulty with the full-blown
theory of a 'symptomatic reading' when applied to a theoretical text
arises in terms of what are the controls on it. It is one thing to read a
complex text with one eye always on the matrix of conceptual premises
and propositions which generates it, gives it what theoretical coherence
it possesses – and also helps us to identify its 'silences', its absences.
'Reading for absence' is certainly one of the principal foundations of a
critical theoretical practice. But it is quite another thing to operate a
'symptomatic reading' like a theoretical guillotine, beheading any
concept which has the temerity to stray from its appointed path. The
line between the two is unfortunately not very well defined.

It is not always easy to differentiate between a 'symptomatic reading'
which enables us to read with effect the theoretical structure of a Marx
text out of those surface formulations where concepts appear in what is
sometimes dubiously called their 'practical state'; and a 'symptomatic
reading' which really provides the cover for so translating these
'practical concepts' into their 'pure' theoretical state that a text can be
made to be 'really' saying whatever it is that the reader has already
determined to find there. *Reading Capital* (Althusser, 1971), which
operates this method in its most rigorous and extreme form, on the one
hand prevents us from an 'innocent' reading of Marx: but is often also
guilty itself of so *transforming* 'what Marx really said' that it – of
course – produces what it first set out to discover. To put it bluntly, if
Marx's 'practical concepts' are systematically raised to a more
theoretical level with the aid of structuralist instruments and concepts
then it is not difficult, in this way, to produce at the end a 'structuralist
Marx'. The question – the extremely important question posed at the
opening of *Reading Capital* – as to what sort of 'structuralist' the
mature Marx really was, cannot be answered in this circular manner.
Althusser himself knows this, since it is *he* who clearly demonstrated (in
For Marx) the necessarily closed circularity of a 'reading' which has its
'answers' already premissed in the form of the questions it poses. He
called this circularity – ideological.

In what follows I shall attempt to avoid *both* the 'innocence' of a
reading which sticks fast to the surface form of an argument; and the
particular form of 'guilt' attached to producing an interpretation which
simply fits my preconceptions. I am aiming at a certain kind of
interrogation of some critical passages in Marx on the question of

classes and class struggle. I link the two together – classes and class struggle – because it is this articulation which concerns me most in this paper, and which has dictated the passages I have chosen to examine. The extremely difficult and complex matter of the theoretical designation of the anatomy of classes *as such* is handled at much greater length in other papers in this symposium, and is left to a brief passage at the end of this paper. I shall be particularly concerned to demonstrate how and why Marx's ideas on classes and class struggle differ, at different periods of his work; and of how they advance. I want, if possible, to reconsider some of the earlier and 'transitional' texts again – many of them having been too swiftly assigned to the conceptual scrap-heap. But I shall certainly want to examine them from the viewpoint of Marx's mature and developed theory: I shall try to look at them, not 'innocently', but *in the light of Capital*. Much of what I shall say ought therefore to be judged, by the reader, in terms of this declared line of departure.

I

The Communist Manifesto was drafted by Marx and Engels for the Communist League 'to make plain to all the true nature of the "spectre" that was supposed to be haunting Europe'. It was published on the eve of the great revolutionary upsurge of 1848 – by the time it appeared, Marx was already in Paris at the invitation of the liberal-radical government which had overthrown Louis-Philippe. It was explicitly designed as a revolutionary tocsin; many if not all, of its simplifications must be understood in that light. By the summer of 1848, the counter-revolution had begun to unroll; Marx and Engels were forced to admit that they had misread the birth-pangs of bourgeois society as its death-knell. Marx changed his mind – about many more things than the speed at which the revolutionary showdown would be enacted. Gwyn Williams (Williams, 1976) has brilliantly demonstrated how this 'break' in perspective – a *political* break – registers inside the *theoretical* structure of one of Marx's most critical texts, *The Eighteenth Brumaire of Louis Bonaparte*. Indeed, without simplifying the connection, we could say that the historical collapse of the 1848 Revolutions produced a theoretical advance of the first order in Marx's understanding of the complex question of classes and their relation to political struggle. One way of assessing the distance he travelled and the discoveries he made can be measured in terms of the *differences* – and convergences – between the way he writes about classes in the *Manifesto* (1847) and the essays on *The Eighteenth Brumaire* and *The Class Struggles In France*, drafted between 1850 and 1852.

The history of all hitherto existing society is the history of class struggles. Freeman and slave, patrician and plebian, lord and serf, guild-master and journeyman, in a word, oppressor and oppressed, stood in constant opposition to one another, carried on an uninterrupted, now hidden, now open fight, a fight that each time ended in a revolutionary reconstruction of society at large, or in the common ruin of the contending classes.

. . . With the development of industry the proletariat not only increases in number; it becomes concentrated in greater masses, its strength grows and it feels that strength more. The various interests are more and more equalised, in proportion as machinery obliterates all distinctions of labour, and nearly everywhere reduces wages to the same low level. The growing competition among the bourgeois . . . makes their livelihood more and more precarious; the collision between individual workmen and individual bourgois takes more and more the character of collision between two classes. Thereupon the workers begin to form combinations (trade unions) against the bourgeois. . . . This organisation of the proletarians into a class, and consequently into a political party, is continually being upset by the competition between the workers themselves. But it ever rises up again, stronger, firmer and mightier. It compels legislative recognition of particular interests of workers, by taking advantage of divisions among the bourgeoisie itself. Thus the Ten Hours Bill in England. (*MESW* (1), pp. 35ff).

What is so fatally seductive about this text is its simplifying revolutionary sweep: its elan, coupled with the optimistic sureness of its grasp on the unrolling, unstoppable tide of revolutionary struggle and proletarian victory; above all, its unmodified sense of historical inevitability. That note sits uneasily with our much refined sense of the revolution's infinitely 'long delay' – and of how much more complex, how less inevitable, its dénouement has proved to be. And this is connected with a rejection of one of the central propositions which appears to power and sustain this unrolling-through-revolution: the progressive simplification of class antagonisms, articulated along a linear path of historical time, into *basically* two hostile camps – bourgeoisie and proletarians, facing one another in a 'process of dissolution of . . . a violent and glaring character'. The whole logic of this part of the text is over-determined by the historical conjuncture in which it was drafted. Undoubtedly, classes are constructed in the text historically, in the simple sense: the dissolution of feudalism; the revolutionary role of the emergent bourgeoisie; 'free competition' and 'free labour' – Marx's two preconditions for the installation of a capitalist mode of production on an expanded scale; the gigantic development of capital's productive capacities; then, industrial and commercial crises; progressive immiseration, class polarisation, revolutionary rupture and overthrow.

This *linearity*, this undisguised historical evolutionism, is interrupted or displaced by the play of, essentially, only a single antagonism: between the developing forces of production, and the 'fettering' relations of production in which the former are embedded. It is this fundamental contradiction which provides the basic punctuation of the class struggle in the capitalist mode. Its course is subject, of course, to delays; but its essential tendency is forwards – towards 'collision'. This is because the two levels are directly harnessed – the class struggle 'matures' as capitalism 'develops'. Indeed, the latter develops and matures the former: capitalism is its own grave-digger. Capitalism thus produces its own 'negation' – the oppressed classes whose rising struggles propel that phase to its conclusion, and drive society forwards to the next stage of its development. Since bourgeois versus proletarians is the most 'universal' of the class struggles to date – the proletariat is the last class to be emancipated; that which 'has nothing to lose but its chains' – the proletarian revolution entails the emancipation of all classes, or the abolition of class society *as such*.

The basic problematic of the *Manifesto* is hardly in doubt. Its presence is luminously rendered in the transparency of the writing – a transparency of style which recapitulates the way the relations and connections dealt with in the text are grasped and driven forwards. It treats classes as 'whole' subjects – collective subjects or actors. It deals with the transposition of the class struggle from the economic to the political level unproblematically. They are interchangeable: the one leads, inexorably, to the other. They are connected by means of what Althusser has called a 'transitive causality'. It treats history as an unfolding sequence of struggles – arranged into epochs, punctuated by *the* class struggle, which is its motor. It conceives a capitalist social formation as, essentially, a simple structure – a structure whose immediate forms may be complex, but whose dynamic and articulation is simple and essentialist: its articulation is basically 'given' by the terms of a single contradiction (forces/relations of production) which unrolls unproblematically from the economic 'base', evenly throughout all its different levels, 'indifferently'. A break at one level therefore gives rise, sooner or later, to a parallel break at the other levels. This has been defined as a 'historicist' conception (Althusser, 1969) because it deals with a social formation as what Althusser calls an 'expressive totality'. There is even, behind this 'historicism', the trace of an earlier problematic: that which conceives of the proletarian revolution as the liberation of all humanity, the 'moment' of the installation of the rule of Reason in History – one which recalls the humanist thrust of, say, the section 'On Communism' of the *1844 Manuscripts*, with its undisguised Feuerbachean and Hegelian overtones. It is a heroic, humanist vision. But it is flawed, both in its substantive predictions and in its mode of conceptualisation.

The most decisive and definitive dismantling of this whole problematic is certainly to be found in Althusser's seminal essay, 'Contradiction And Over-determination', in *For Marx*. The *Manifesto* must now be read in the light of that intervention. Briefly, in it, Althusser argues that in the concrete analysis of any specific historical moment, although the principal contradiction of the capitalist mode of production – that between the forces of production and the 'fettering' relations of production – provides the 'final' determinacy, the terms of this contradiction, alone, are not sufficient for analysing the way *different levels of class struggle* lead to a revolutionary rupture. Because the levels of a social formation are not neatly aligned in the way the *Manifesto* suggests, contradictions do not immediately and unmediatedly unroll from the economic base, producing a rupture or break at all the different levels simultaneously. Indeed, as Lenin indicated with respect to 1917, the crucial question is rather how 'absolutely dissimilar currents, absolutely heterogeneous class interests, absolutely contrary political and social strivings have merged . . . in a strikingly "harmonious" manner' as the result of an 'extremely unique historical situation'. These dissimilar currents cannot, then, be reduced to the determinacy of the 'laws' of the economic base. 'The Capital-Labour contradiction is never simple, but always specified by the historically concrete forms and circumstances in which it is exercised. It is specified by the forms of the superstructure . . . by the internal and external historical situation . . . many of these phenomena deriving from the "law of uneven development" in the Leninist sense' (Althusser, 1969).

This requires us to conceive of different contradictions, each with its own specificity, its own tempo of development, internal history, and its own conditions of existence – at once 'determined and determining': in short, it poses the question of the relative autonomy and the specific effectivity of the different levels of a social formation. If this is to be combined with the cardinal principle of Marxism – that without which it is theoretically indistinguishable from any other 'sociology' – namely, 'determination in the last instance by the (economic) mode of production', then a decisive turn in the relations of forces in a social formation cannot be adequately 'thought' in terms of a *reduction* of all the secondary contradictions to the terms of the principal contradiction. In short, Marxism requires a form of determinacy which is *not* equivalent to an economic reductionism. The 'merging' of these 'heterogeneous currents', Althusser suggests, is better 'thought', not as a reduction but as a *complex effect* – an accumulation of all the instances and effects, a merger, a rupture – an 'over-determination'. It follows from this argument that a social formation is not a 'totality' of the essentialist type, in which there is a simple 'identity' between its different levels, with the superstructural levels the mere 'epiphenomena' of the objective laws governing 'the economic base'. It is, rather, a unity of a necessarily complex type – an 'ensemble' which is always the result of many determinations: a unity, moreover which is characterised by its *unevenness*.

In his 1857 *Introduction* to the *Grundrisse* Marx argued that, though Capital, in its prolonged circuit, requires both production, distribution and exchange, these must not be thought as 'equivalents', but as different 'moments' of a circuit, *articulated into* a 'unity' – a unity which does not efface their necessary differences but must be 'thought' rather 'in terms of their differences'. And though 'production' does exert a final determinacy over the circuit as a whole, each 'moment' has its own determinateness, plays its necessary, non-reducible role in the self-expanding value of capital, obeying its own conditions of existence. The relation, specifically, of the economic to the political must, similarly, be conceptualised as articulated into a unity, through their necessary differences and displacements. There is therefore *no necessary immediate correspondence* between the 'economic' and the 'political' constitution of classes. The terms in which their 'complex unity' could be thought, of course, remained to be developed. But there can be little doubt that these developments decisively mark out as radically different the terrain of Marx's subsequent work from that so lucidly prescribed in the *Manifesto*.

Important as it is to mark the line which separates the phase of Marx's thought which finds a definitive statement in the *Manifesto* from his subsequent development, it is also necessary to remind ourselves of what cannot be left behind – of what has already been gained, what is irreducible in it. This becomes clearer provided we detach the *Manifesto* a little from its immediate location, and reconsider its 'advances', as I have tried to phrase it, 'in the light of *Capital*'. The declaration that 'the history of all hitherto existing society is the history of class struggles', for example, is as fundamental to Marxism as it was to appear a 'startling premiss' when first enunciated. Marxism is unthinkable without it. The emphasis on 'classes' there is almost as fundamental as the emphasis on 'struggles'. The brief articulation of this proposition which immediately follows – freemen and slave, lord and serf, bourgeois and proletarian – though in no sense an *adequate* account of the complex class structures of the modes of production to which they refer, (and therefore the site of a continuing difficulty) – is an absolutely necessary starting point. The idea that 'men' first appear as biological individuals, or as the 'bare individuals' of market society, and only then are coalesced into classes – class as, so to speak, a secondary formation – is not a reading supportable from this text or anything in Marx which follows it. This premiss therefore foreshadows the many later passages in which Marx dethrones the apparently natural and obvious reference back to 'individuals' as the basis for a theory of classes.

From the standpoint of Marxism, 'men' are always preconstituted by the antagonistic class relations into which they are cast. Historically, they are always articulated, not in their profound and unique individuality, but *by* 'the ensemble of social relations' – that is as the supports for class relations. It is this prior constitution which produces, under specific conditions, as its *results*, a specific type of individuality: the possessive individual of bourgeois political theory, the needy individual of market society, the contracting individual of the society of 'free labour'. Outside these relations, the individual – this 'Robinson Crusoe' of classical political economy, self-sufficient in a world surveyed only from the standpoint of 'his' needs and wants – which has formed the natural, de-historicised point of origin of bourgeois society and theory, is not a possible theoretical starting point at all. It is only the 'product of many determinations'. The history of its production, Marx once remarked (in *Capital* I, p. 715) 'is written in the annals of mankind in letters of blood and fire'. As he subsequently argued:

Society is not merely an aggregate of individuals; it is the sum of relations in which individuals stand to one another. It is as though someone were to say that, from the point of view of society, slaves and citizens do not exist; they are all men. In fact, this is rather what they are outside society. Being a slave or a citizen is a socially determined relation between individual A and individual B. Individual A is not as such a slave. He is only a slave in and through society (*Grundrisse*, p. 265).

Like all its predecessors, the capitalist process of production proceeds under definite material conditions which are, however, simultaneously the bearers of definite social relations entered into by individuals in the process of reproducing their life. Those conditions, like these relations, are on the one hand pre-requisites, on the other hand results . . . of the capitalist process of production; they are produced and reproduced by it (*Capital* III, pp. 818–19).

Almost everything which passes for a sort of sociological 'common sense' about social classes is contradicted and forbidden by those formulations: and their essential point is already implicit in the *Manifesto*.

Second, there is the premiss which Marx himself noted as the nub of his own contribution (Marx to Weydemeyer, 5 March 1852: *MESC*, p. 69) and which is reaffirmed again by Marx and Engels in their joint Preface to the 1872 German edition of the *Manifesto*: the premiss that 'the existence of classes is only bound up with particular phases in the development of production'. It is the conditions and relations of production, made specific to different phases in the contradictory development of capital, which provides the basic and essential framework for a Marxist theory of classes. It is this premiss which divides Marxism as a 'scientific' theory from all previous and subsequent forms of Utopian Socialism. Henceforth the class struggle was no longer a moral assertion about the inhumanity of the capitalist system, nor was capitalism's destruction projected on to the system from the outside by an exercise of will or hope.

Capitalism, in this sense, produces and reproduces itself *as* an antagonistic structure of class relations: it remorselessly divides the 'population', again and again into its antagonistic classes. Note, at the same time, that it is the phases in the development of the *mode of production* which provides the necessary, though not the sufficient, condition for a Marxist theory of classes: it is not 'the economic' in some more obvious sense, which 'determines'. Marx is absolutely consistent about this, from the first formulations of the question in *The German Ideology*, through to the end. But so powerful is the grasp of bourgeois common-sense, and so persistently does it return to exert its influence even at the heart of Marxist theory itself, that it is worth repeating. It is the material and social relations within which men produce and reproduce their material conditions of existence which 'determines' – *how* remains to be elucidated. The unequal distribution of economic wealth, goods and power, which forms the basis for a 'socio-economic' conception of 'social classes' is, for Marx, not the basis but the *result* of the *prior* distribution of the agents of capitalist production into classes and class relations, and the prior distribution of the means of production as between its 'possessors' and its 'dispossessed'.

The simplification of classes, which appears to be a fundamental thesis of the *Manifesto*, is also not as simple an argument as it at first appears. In arguing that, under capitalism bourgeois versus proletarians is the fundamental form of the class struggle, the *Manifesto* does not – as is sometimes supposed – neglect the presence of other classes and class fractions. Indeed, it contains a summary judgement on the revolutionary potential of *inter alia* 'the lower middle classes, the small manufacturer, the shopkeeper, the artisan, the peasant' as well as 'the dangerous class, the social scum', from which Marx never departed. What it argues is that 'of all the classes that stand face to face with the bourgeoisie today, the proletariat alone is the really revolutionary class'. This is a difficult point, requiring further examination.

Marx comes to the assertion on the basis of the objective position which the proletariat has in a mode of production, based on the latter's expropriation from the means of production and the exploitation of its labour power. In *this* sense the proposition stands – the revolutionary *position* of the proletariat being, in this sense, 'given' (specified) by its location in a specific mode. This does, however, tend to treat the proletariat as an unfractured and undifferentiated 'class subject' – a subject with a role *in* history but no internal, contradictory history of its own, at least within the capitalist epoch. This is a premiss which Marx subsequently modified and which we must reject. But the passage could also be read as if it asserted that, *because* the proletariat has an objectively revolutionary *position* in the economic structure of capitalist production, *therefore* it also and always must exhibit empirically a revolutionary political consciousness and form of political organisation. It is just this further 'move' which Lukács makes in *History and Class Consciousness*; and when he is obliged to recognise that this proletariat does not 'empirically' always live up to its appointed form of consciousness, he treats it 'abstractly' as if this is its ascribed destiny – its 'potential consciousness' – from which its actual, concrete historical divergences are but temporary lapses. The enormous historical problem, for Marxism, of the 'economism' of trade union consciousness, and of the containment of the Western European working-class movements within the confines of social democratic reformism, cannot be systematically elucidated from this position. We come back, then, to one of the critical weaknesses – it recurs in one form or another throughout the text – of the *Manifesto*: a weakness which can now be summarily stated.

The *Manifesto* is correct in its (obviously and necessarily schematic) discussion of the economic constitution of classes in terms of the phases of development of the mode of production. But it is fatally flawed in treating, systematically, the relation between the economic and the political. To this question the *Manifesto* either returns an unsatisfactory answer (i.e. they are more or less aligned, more or less 'corresponding'); or it leaves a *space*, a gap, through which the abstract error of a Lukácsean historicism constantly escapes. In short, all that is necessary to think the specificity of the political class struggle and its relation to the economic level – on which our ability to expound 'the ensemble' as a whole depends – is not yet present as usable concepts in Marx's thought. These further concepts are, indeed, *forced into discovery* by the historical and political conjuncture they were required to explain: the collapse of the 1848 revolutions. Thus, precisely, their clearest and most substantial formulation occurs in the essays and studies which immediately follow – the writings on France, especially, more fleetingly (and less satisfactorily) the asides on Britain: texts which, so to speak, appear in the light of theoretical reflection and clarification cast by a moment of revolutionary defeat. Here we are on the terrain of real discoveries, of a theoretically revolutionary *break-through*. This break-through occurs 'in thought', certainly: but it can hardly be adequately understood as 'epistemological'.

Still, we have not fully plumbed the depth of that brilliantly-surfaced text, the *Manifesto*. Why and how did Marx and Engels envisage the 'simplification' of classes (with its profound consequences for decyphering the rhythm of the class struggle) to be *implicit* in the unfolding of capitalist development?

II

It is the increasing size and scale of capitalist production which precipitates this 'simplification'. The circumstances which, first, produce the proletariat, then develop it, then drive all the intermediary class strata into its growing ranks are worth briefly detailing: (a) the formation of a class, expropriated from the ownership of the means of production, with only its labour power to sell, exposed to the 'vicissitudes of competition and all the fluctuations of the market'; (b) the division of labour consequent on the extensive use of machinery which 'deskills' the worker, reducing him to an appendage of the machine; (c) the growing exploitation of labour power 'whether by prolongation of the working day in a given time or by increased speed of the machinery, etc.'; (d) the organisation of labour into an 'industrial army' in factory conditions under the command of capital's 'officers and sergeants'; (e) the *dilution* of labour through the lowering of the value of labour power – the employment, at lower wages, of women and children; (f) the exposure of the class to exploitation in the market for subsistence goods – by the landlord, the shop-keeper, the pawn-broker. In this context arises (g) the thesis that the lower strata of the middle class 'sink gradually into the proletariat' – partly through their losing battle with (h) large-scale, concentrated 'big' capital. The intermediary strata are what Gramsci would call 'subaltern' fractions of the middle classes. They are intrinsically conservative, reactionary in outlook – trying to 'roll back the wheel of history'. They are or become 'revolutionary' only face to face with their 'impending transfer into the proletariat' – their 'proletarianisation'.

The attentive reader will recognise at once that all of these sketchy ideas reappear, and are subject to a major development, above all in Marx's seminal Chapter XV on 'Machinery and Modern Industry' in *Capital* I. The formation, historically, of a class of 'free labour', with nothing to sell but its labour-power, out of the matrix of feudal relations, is constantly returned to in *Capital* as its 'historic basis'. The progressive reduction of the worker to an 'appendage of the machine' is central to Marx's description of the capitalist labour process, and to his qualitative distinction between the phase of 'machinery' and the phase of 'modern industry'. The growing exploitation of labour power foreshadows the critical distinction in *Capital* between Absolute (the prolongation of the working day) and Relative (the increase of the ratio of 'dead' to 'living' labour) surplus value. The growing hierarchisation and 'despotism' of capital's command leads on to Marx's distinction between the 'formal' and the 'real' subsumption of labour. The 'dilution' of skilled labour and the formation of a 'reserve army' are two of the critical 'counter-acting tendencies' to the tendency of the rate of profit to fall, discussed both in *Capital* I (for example, Chapter XXV) and again in *Capital* III, where the processes leading to the growing concentration and centralisation of capitals are more fully described. In this context, also there arises the description of the emergence of the modern 'collective worker' and the first hints at the *expansion* of the *new* intermediary classes, consequent on a developing division of labour, as the older petty-bourgeoisie and its material basis in 'small' and trading capital is eroded. In the context of this major theoretical development, the sketchy outline of the *Manifesto*, which contains little but an *indication* of how the organisation of capitalist production provides the basis for this *formation* and *recomposition* of classes, is both expanded and transformed. Again, both continuities and the breaks necessary for their theoretical development must be observed.

When in *Capital* Marx sets out to resume, in a condensed form, the general overall tendency of this whole development, the terms he employs are *strikingly similar* to those he employed in the *Manifesto*.

One has only to turn to the summary review contained in the brief Chapter XXXII of *Capital* I to hear again the familiar phrases:

At a certain stage of development it brings forth the material agencies of its own dissolution. From that moment new forces and new passions spring up in the bosom of society: but the old organisation fetters them and keeps them down. . . . As soon as this process of transformation has sufficiently decomposed the old society from top to bottom, as soon as the labourers are turned into proletarians, their means of labour into capital, as soon as the capitalist mode of production stands on its own feet, then the further socialisation of labour . . . takes a new form. . . . This expropriation is accomplished by the action of the immanent laws of capitalist production itself, by the centralisation of capital. . . . Hand in hand with this centralisation, or this expropriation of many capitals by few, develop, on an ever-extending scale, the cooperative form of the labour-process, the conscious technical application of science, the methodological cultivation of the soil, the transformation of the instruments of labour into instruments of labour only usable in common, the economising of all means of production by their use as the means of production of combined, socialised labour, the entanglement of all peoples in the net of the world market . . . but with this too grows the revolt of the working-class, a class always increasing in numbers, and disciplined, united, organised by the very mechanism of the process of capitalist production itself (*Capital* I, 714–15).

This is the echo, the 'voice' of the *Manifesto*, inside *Capital*.

But side by side with this résumé, we must set the detail, but more significantly the *method*, by which the simple sketch of the *Manifesto* is transformed into the terms and concepts of *Capital*'s investigation. It is impossible within the scope of this paper to provide the 'reading' which would substantiate in detail the nature of this theoretical transformation. But some examples can be taken in order to demonstrate how the sketch of the process in the *Manifesto* – structured largely on a linear development, punctuated by the rising tempo of class struggle – is *thoroughly transformed*, in its reworking in *Capital*, by really setting to work the concept of *contradiction* and the notion of dialectical development.

Two examples will have to suffice. In the opening section of Chapter XV, Marx established the technical difference between the nature of the instruments of production (and the consequent division of labour in the labour process itself) which characterises the *first* phase of capitalist development – the era of Machinery – and that further qualitative development – 'machinery organised into a system', where the machine 'uses' the worker rather than the reverse – which marks out the period of 'Modern Industry'. In the section on 'The Factory' Marx then explores the complex and contradictory effects of this transformation of capitalism's material basis. He comments, *inter alia*, on the decomposition of the traditional skills of the class, as these skills are increasingly 'passing over' into the machine itself: here, he notes, the *tendency* towards the equalisation and reduction of skills 'to one and the same level of every kind of work'. But this has consequences, at once, for the *social* organisation of production: it brings in its train the recomposition of the elements of production into 'the head workman' and his 'mere attendants': and, alongside this, the new 'superior class of workmen, some of them scientifically educated' who look after the whole of the machinery itself and repair it.

As the machine begins to dictate the organisation of the labour process, it brings further contradictory developments with it: the greater ease of substituting one labour force for another; the introduction of continuous production and the shift system (the 'relay system'); the dilution of labour and the erosion of traditional skills born of an earlier division of labour – 'traditional habits' now 'systematically remoulded'. In the annexation of worker to the machine, the systematic 'pumping dry' of living labour by dead labour proceeds at an enormous pace – the 'special skills of each individual factory operator vanishes as an infinitesimal quantity before the science, the gigantic physical forces and the mass of labour that are embodied in the factory mechanism'. But this has further consequences, too, for the nature of factory discipline, hierarchy and command – redividing workers into 'operatives and overlookers' (the 'private soldiers and sergeants of an industrial army') – and for the administration of a more detailed and coercive labour regime. Dr Andrew Ure, the 'poet' of Modern Industry, himself saw how the revolution in the means of production both *required* and *made possible* the withdrawal of any process requiring parti- cular skill and dexterity from the 'cunning workman . . . prone to irregularities' to the 'self-regulating mechanism' which even the child can superintend. Thus the 'technical' revolution in the means of production produces an unlooked for effect in the regulation of labour and the repression of the strikes and other 'periodic revolts' of the working class against its conditions of life. Again, as Marx, quoting

Ure, observes: when 'capital enlists science into her service, the refractory hand of labour will always be taught docility'.

In this Section alone we see how what, in the *Manifesto*, appears to be organised around a simple antagonism, is articulated into a complex and contradictory one: the necessary terms are *effects*, not intended, which nevertheless have contradictory outcomes: effects at *levels* where no result was calculated: *tendencies*, immediately cross-cut by their opposite: advances which produce, elsewhere regressive results. Above all, what was in the earlier text represented as an essentially homogeneous force – the proletariat – is now itself constantly and ceaselessly acted upon, redefined, recomposed, 'remoulded' by the operation of capital's contradictory law. Already in the *Manifesto* Marx had foreseen how the growing cohesion of the proletariat, in the conditions of factory labour, was constantly interrupted by the tendency towards 'competition between workers'. But it is only when the process of development which lays the foundation for that growing cohesion is investigated in depth that we can see *why* it is that capital produces, of necessity, *both* the massification and the 'simplification' of labour, as one of its tendencies; but also, equally 'necessarily', the internal divisions between skilled and the unskilled, the distribution of skills into different branches of production, as 'Modern Industry' seizes on them and transforms them *unevenly*: how the 'dilution' of the traditional work-force by the employment on a large scale of women and children (a development made possible only by the revolution in the nature of the labour process itself) sets one group of workers against another, introducing as a further contradiction 'the natural differences of age and sex' – i.e. the sexual division of labour into its social division: and how capital comes to be in a position to exploit these new elements in the division of labour (or the parallel one between supervisors, the 'superior class of workmen' and the machine-minders) to its political advantage. In short how the production of two, opposite *tendencies* in capital's contradictory development decisively *intervenes* between any simple notion of the 'inevitable cohesion of the proletariat' and its actual realisation under the new conditions of capital's historic organisation.

Something absolutely central about the form and character of the class struggle under modern conditions of production is already present in the deceptively simple remark, by Marx, that:

So far as division of labour reappears in the factory it is primarily a dis-tribution of the workmen among the specialised machines; and of masses of workmen, not however organised into groups, among the various departments of the factory, in each of which they work at a number of similar machines placed together; their cooperation therefore is only simple. The organised group, peculiar to manufacture, is replaced by the connexion between the head workman and his few assistants (*Capital*, vol. 1, p. 396).

This tendency does not obliterate the earlier one: it represents both the expanding base for the 'socialisation of labour' and the technical interdependence of the various branches of capitalist production: as well as the social basis for the formation of a modern proletariat. The development of capitalism reproduces *both* tendencies at once: in short, in driving itself forward through one of its 'technical' limits, in overcoming one of the material barriers to its revolutionising self-expansion, capital produces new contradictions at a higher level of development. Its advance – quite contrary to the dominant impression of the *Manifesto* – is, in the *full* sense, dialectical.

We can see this at work in another instance, where also there are apparently straight 'echoes' of the *Manifesto*. Marx noted in that text the two 'paths' open to capital – prolongation of the working day, and the 'increase of the work exacted in a given time . . . the increased speed of machinery, etc'. He also noted, but in another context, the growing political strength of the proletariat — 'it ever rises up again, stronger firmer, mightier' – compelling a recognition of the 'particular interests of the workers'; in this latter context he cites the 'Ten Hour bill'. Again, it is striking to observe how deeply and thoroughly these ideas are transformed as they reappear in *Capital*. The enlarged application of machinery has the effect of increasing the productivity of labour — 'shortening the working-time required in the production of a commodity'. But it also has the effect of reducing the resistance of the workers to the prolongation of the working day. Here, at once, is a contradiction, 'since of the two factors of the surplus-value created by a given amount of capital, one, the rate of surplus-value, cannot be increased except by diminishing the other, the number of workmen'. The effects are, therefore, as contradictory as they are 'unconscious' (p. 407, fn. i). If it extends the working day, 'changes the method of labour, as also the character of the social working organism, in such a manner as to break down all opposition to this tendency', it also 'produces,

partly by opening out to the capitalist new strata of the working class
. . . partly by setting free the labourers it supplants, a surplus working
population'. It is this unfettered exploitation of labour power which
provokes 'a reaction' on the part of a section of the ruling class – a
reaction leading to 'divisions among the bourgeoisie itself' which the
workers' struggle takes advantage of, forcing through the Factory
legislation, with its statutory limits to the working day. Marx
subsequently notes that the capitalists oppose this limit, politically,
vigorously: they declare production to be 'impossible' under such
conditions. Yet it is precisely the imposition of this limit – which 'the
surging revolt of the working class compelled [on] Parliament' – which
drives capital forward to 'raising the productive power of the workman,
so as to enable him to produce more in a given time with the same
expenditure of labour'. This is the enormous – the uneven and
unplanned – threshold which capital crosses, from the epoch of
Absolute to that of Relative surplus value.

Its effects are immense: the rise in the organic composition of capital;
the lowering of the value component of every commodity; the
intensification of the labour process; the 'filling up of the pores of the
working day'; the 'increasing tension of labour power'; the speed-up of
the production process; the great stimulus to technical advance and the
application of science as a material force; and the gain in the
administration of a regime of 'regularity, uniformity, order, continuity'
in labour – these are only *some* of the consequences Marx outlines. By
1858, Marx notes, the Factory Inspector is reporting that 'the great
improvements made in machines of every kind have raised their
productive power very much . . . Without any doubt, the shortening of
the hours of labour . . . gave the impulse to these improvements'.
Towards the end of Chapter XV, Marx returns again to the complex
outcome of the mid-century Factory legislation, dealing now more fully
both with its technical and its social (education, children, the family)
consequences. Thus what appears in the *Manifesto* as a simple
disconnection between the levels of the mode of production and of
political struggle, is brought together into a contradictory 'unity': a
unity which shows how, while the law of value obtains, capital
advances, blindly, unconsciously – as Brecht would say, 'from its bad
side': how it is impelled to advance itself by contravening the very limits
and barriers it establishes for itself: how its 'political' consciousness is

often at variance with its inner drive and necessities. It illustrates vividly capital's powers of *recuperation*: how it constantly is forced to weave together its own contradictory impulses into forms of social and economic organisation which it can bend and force to advance its own 'logic'. It shows how, in order to master the divisions of interest within its own ranks, and above all to master and contain within its framework those 'particular' advances which the working class is able to force upon it, capital develops a different *repertoire*: it discovers new 'solutions'. Any idea that the 'logic of capital' is a simple and straightforward functional 'unfolding', or that its logic is one which can be separated from the 'logic of class struggle' – two disconnected threads – is definitively disposed of in this Chapter.

Out of this historical-analytic exposition Marx detaches the seminal theoretical argument, which is then presented (in the following chapter) in its 'purer' theoretical form: the concepts of 'The Production of Absolute and of Relative Surplus Value'. The whole tendential direction is thus concisely summarised: the 'general extension of factory legislation to all trades for the purpose of protecting the working class' – the outcome of an immediate political struggle – also 'hastens on the general conversion of numerous isolated small industries into a few combined industries . . . it therefore accelerates the concentration of capital and the exclusive predominance of the factory system'. It 'destroys ancient and transitional forms behind which the domination of capital is still in part concealed, and replaces them by the direct and open sway of capital; but thereby it also generalises the direct opposition to this sway.' It enforces uniformity, regularity, order and economy, and provides the spur to technical improvement, the intensity of labour and the 'competition of machinery with the worker'. It destroys the material basis of petty and domestic production. 'By maturing the material conditions and the combination on a social scale of the processes of production, it matures the contradictions and antagonisms of the capitalist form of production' (*Capital* I, p. 503). If this appears to make a last-hour return to the terrain of the *Manifesto*, it is only in so far as the contradictory double-thrust of capitalist development and its intrinsically antagonistic nature lies at the heart of both conceptions. From the vantage point of *Capital*, the so-called 'simplification of classes and the class struggle' – or what we must now call the *complex simplification* of classes and the logic of class struggle

within the 'logic' of capital's historic development – has been
thoroughly and irreversibly transformed. In terms of the Marxist
'theory of classes', we have entered quite new territory.

III

As we have seen, one of the critical points left in an unsatisfactory state
by the *Manifesto* is the relations between the economic and the political
aspects of class struggle. Marx does pose the question of 'this
organisation of the proletarians into a class . . . and consequently into a
party': as if the political aspects were simply a more advanced form of
the 'economic', requiring no alteration of terms or extension of
conceptual framework. In *The German Ideology*, Marx says of the
capitalist class that 'the separate individuals form a class in so far as
they have to carry on a common battle against another class; otherwise
they are on hostile terms with one another as competitors' (*German
Ideology*, p. 69). In *The Poverty of Philosophy* Marx speaks of Utopian
Socialism as typical of a period in which 'the proletariat is not
sufficiently developed to constitute itself into a class' and consequently,
'the very struggle of the proletariat with the bourgeoisie has not yet
assumed a political character' (*MECW*, vol. 6, p. 177). He calls the
proletariat 'this mass' which is already a class in opposition to capital
but not yet a class for itself'. In *The Eighteenth Brumaire*, Marx writes:

In so far as millions of families live under economic conditions of existence that
separate their mode of life, their interests and their culture from those of other
classes and put them in hostile opposition to the latter, they form a class. In so
far as there is merely a local interconnection among these small-holding
peasants and the identity of their interests begets no community, no national
bond, no political organisation amongst them, they do not form a class. They
are consequently incapable of enforcing their class interests in their own name.

In 1871, in a Letter to Friedrich Bolte, which touches again the Factory
legislation discussed above, Marx writes:

The ultimate object of the political movement of the working class is, of course,
the conquest of political power for this class, and this naturally requires that the
organisation of the working class, and the organisation which arises from its
economic struggles should previously reach a certain level of development. On

the other hand, however, every movement in which the working class as a *class* confronts the ruling classes and tries to constrain them by pressure from without is a political movement. For instance the attempt by strikes, etc., in a particular factory or even in a particular trade to compel individual capitalists to reduce the working day, is a purely economic movement. On the other hand, the movement to force through an eight hour, etc., *law* is a *political* movement. And in this way, out of the separate economic movements of the workers there grows up everywhere a *political* movement, that is to say, a *class*, movement, with the object of enforcing its interests in a general form, in a form possessing general, socially coercive force. While these movements presuppose a certain degree of previous organisation, they are in turn equally a means of developing this organisation (23 November 1871, *MESC*, pp. 254–5).

Marx was writing here to clarify certain theses of the General Council of the International whose Rules he had formulated. A few days later Engels was to write in very similar terms for a very similar purpose to the Turin newspaper, *Il Proletario Italiano*:

The economical emancipation of the working classes is . . . the great end to which every political movement ought to be subordinated as a means . . . in the struggle of the working class its economic movement and its political action are indissolubly united (29 November 1871, *MESC*, p. 255).

Here we find Marx and Engels rethinking precisely what is too simply proposed and glossed in the *Manifesto*: the necessary displacements as well as the conjunctures in the relation between the political and economic forms of the class struggle. The span of time is a lengthy one – from *The Poverty of Philosophy* to the Paris Commune; and in that period Marx's thought on this critical topic underwent what has been called 'further fluctuations' (Poulantzas, 1973, p. 58). These 'fluctuations' need to be treated with care.

The distinction drawn in the *Poverty of Philosophy* passage between class 'in itself' and class 'for itself' has, subsequently, hardened into a sort of pat formula. It appears to pose the economic/political relation in an incorrect manner. It suggests that there comes a moment when the proletariat as a whole develops the form of revolutionary class consciousness ascribed for it in its given, objective economic determination; and that only then does the class exist *at all* at the level of political struggle. We have indicated earlier the weakness which lies behind this too-neat bifurcation: which seems exclusively to reserve for such a moment of fulfilled consciousness the ascription 'political class struggle'; which derives it too neatly from the economic determinations of class; which makes the achievement of an 'autonomous' form of consciousness the only test of the political existence of a class; and which treats classes as unified historical subjects.

The 'in itself/for itself' distinction *is* useful as a way of defining different moments and forms of class consciousness, and perhaps even as a very rough way of marking the development out of a 'corporate' form of class struggle. But this would in fact require us to develop Marx's passing observation in a manner which is at odds with where it is pointing in this passage: for the distinction between 'corporate' and what Marx later calls a struggle which possesses 'general, socially coercive force' is *not* a distinction between the presence/absence of political struggle and its 'appropriate' forms of class consciousness, but precisely the opposite: a distinction between *two different forms* of the class struggle, two modes of class consciousness, each with its own determinate conditions in the material circumstances of the classes under capitalism. As both Marx and Engels observed, and as Lenin remarked even more extensively, working class reformism and 'trade union consciousness' – or what Lenin in *What Is To Be Done?* calls specifically 'working class bourgeois politics' (*CW*, vol. 5, p. 437) – has its own conditions of existence, its own material base in the economic conditions of the working class under capitalism: far from being a level or form of class struggle, so to speak 'below' the horizon of politics, it could be said to be the natural (or as Lenin called it, the 'spontaneous') form of working class struggle, in conditions where the means of raising that struggle to its more 'general' form are absent. But what those conditions might be, through which the forms of economic and political struggle can be heightened to their 'general' form, is not given in the in itself/for itself distinction.

The Letter to Bolte, on the other hand, has quite a different purchase. The phrase 'the conquest of political power for this class' has behind it the force of Marx's observations about the necessity of breaking the political power of the state erected by the bourgeoisie; and his stress on the 'dictatorship of the proletariat', which arose from his analysis of the Paris Commune, was embodied in *The Civil War in France*. More interestingly, the terms 'economic' and 'political' appear to be used, here, to designate *where*, in any specific conjuncture, the class struggle appears to have pertinent effects. The organisation by the proletariat within production to constrain capital's efforts to intensify the exploitation of labour by prolongation of the working day is defined as an 'economic movement' which attempts to modify the law governing the limitation of the working day (whose object must therefore be the bourgeois state itself) and constitutes a 'political movement'. Here, everything is translated to the level of the concrete conjuncture of a specific historical moment in which the class struggle 'takes effect'. Every trace of automatism in the movements between these two levels has been obliterated. What all the passages quoted put on the agenda, however, is the question of what the further conditions are, and what are the forms, by means of which the antagonistic relations of production of the capitalist mode can appear at, and have such pertinent effects in, the 'theatre' of politics. It is above all in the *Class Struggles in France* and in *The Eighteenth Brumaire* that the concepts begin to emerge which enable us to grasp the sources and the mechanisms of the 'relative autonomy' of the political level of the class struggle from the economic.

The first sections of *The Class Struggles in France* were composed in the immediate aftermath of 1848. Though already convinced that the proletariat was still too 'immature' to carry the day, this part of Marx's analysis is concentrated by the way the bourgeois political forces are driven by their own internal contradictions to destroy the basis of their own 'mature' political rule – universal suffrage – and consequently come gradually to confront the stark alternatives: retreat under the protection of Napoleon's bayonets, or proletarian revolution. The final Section was, however, drafted and published later: and there is a major and irreversible 'break' between the two perspectives. Fernbach has called it 'perhaps the most important [break] during his entire political work as a communist'. The nature of that break is resumed by Gwyn Williams: 'In the summer of 1850 Marx returned to his economic studies which were to immerse him in the British Museum for so many years. He came to the conclusion that the 1848 cycle of revolution had been set in train by a particular crisis in the new capitalist society . . . that the return of prosperity made a new wave of revolutions exceedingly unlikely and, more important, that no proletarian revolution was possible on the continent until capitalist economy and capitalist relations of production had been much more fully developed. . . . His new perspective was grounded in a much fuller and more structural analysis, the analysis which was in fact to reach its climax in *Capital* seventeen years later' (Williams, 1976, p. 112).

The difference – most profoundly, then, registered in the analysis Marx offers in *The Eighteenth Brumaire* – does *not* differ from the schemas of the *Manifesto* in the sense of emphasising 'politics' at the expense of the 'objective conditions' constituted by the level of development of the forces and relations of capitalism. Quite the reverse. The objective determinations and the limits on what solutions were, and were not 'possible' at the political level are, in the later work, if anything *more* rigorously formulated, more structurally conceived and more systematically enforced than in the earlier texts. The elaboration of the 'practical concepts' of the political, for which *The Eighteenth Brumaire* is justly famous, is structured, through and through, by this unrelenting application of the 'determinations' which objective conditions place over the political resolutions. What Marx breaks with is any lingering assumption that the two levels exactly correspond: that the terms and contents of the one are fully given in the conditions and limits of the other. What he does, in the detailed and provocative tracing out of the forms which the class struggle assumes in what Gramsci calls 'its passage to the level of the complex superstructure' (Gramsci, 1971), is to put into place, for the first time, those concepts which alone enable us to 'think' *the specificity of the political*.

Briefly, then, in its overall tendency and trajectory, the crisis of 1851 is fundamentally and decisively over-determined by the objective development of French capitalism. It is this which establishes the outer limits, the determinations, the horizon within which the forms of the political arise and appear. Relatively, the French social formation is still at an early stage of its capitalist development. The proletariat, with its slogans and demands, is already 'on stage'; but it cannot as yet play the decisive role, and, above all, it cannot play an autonomous role. The bourgeoisie is already fully formed, articulated in politics through its major fractions, each fraction playing now one, now another of the political parties and factions, trying now one, now another of the available solutions. But *its* historic role is not anywhere near completion: above all, it has by no means as yet 'netted' those classes which arose in earlier modes of production within its hegemonic sway. The bourgeoisie is therefore not yet in a position where it can, on its own feet and in its own terms, lay hold of French society and 'conform' its civil and political structures to the needs of the developing capitalist mode. The Republic thus totters from one unstable coalition to another; it runs through the entire repertoire of republican and democratic forms – constitutional assembly, parliamentary democracy, bourgeois-republican, republican-socialist. Each 'form' represents the attempt by a fraction – always in a temporary *alliance* – to secure political hegemony. As each alliance is exhausted or defeated, the social base to a possible solution narrows: in each the proletariat is either a pertinent but subordinate partner, or – as the end approaches – the force which is isolated. Finally, when all the possible solutions are exhausted, the unstable equilibrium of political forces on stage falls into the keeping of Napoleon Bonaparte, who 'would like to appear as the patriarchal benefactor of all classes' but only because he has already *broken them*: 'Above all things, France requires tranquillity'.

We must restrict ourselves here to only two aspects of this demonstration: the question of the classes and their political 'forms of appearance', and the problem of the 'determination in the last instance' of the economic mode of production over the forms and outcomes of the political struggle.

The first thing to notice is that, though the entire exposition is framed with the structural analysis of the fundamental classes of the capitalist mode constantly in mind as its *analytic framework* – it is this which provides the whole, dazzling, dramatic narrative with its mastering logic – there are no 'whole classes' on stage here. The proletariat is the class which is most frequently treated as a 'bloc' – and even here the designation of a specific and critical role to the 'lumpen-proletariat' intersects the tendency to present the proletariat in the clash of positions as an 'integral' force. For capital, Marx always distinguishes its dominant *fractions* – 'big landed property'; 'high finance, large-scale industry, large-scale trade'; capital's 'two great interests', 'financial aristocracy', 'industrial bourgeoisie', etc. The petty-bourgeoisie – 'a transitional class in which the interests of the two classes meet and become blurred' – is given, in fact, a pivotal role and position. When Marx comes finally to the class characterization of Napoleon, he signals the presence of a class which was in fact a declining historical force – and differentiates its key fraction: the 'small peasant proprietors'.

The second thing is to note that none of these fractions ever function on the political stage in isolation. The key concept which connects the particular class fractions with the political and constitutional forms is the term – or, rather, the shifting and constantly reconstituted terms of the alliance or class bloc. The first constitutional form of the 'crisis' is that of the *bourgeois republic*. The republic is hoisted to power by the June insurrection of the Paris proletariat: but though this is the class which bears the brunt of the struggle, it is a *subordinate* party to the alliance. Temporarily, the *leading fractions* in the alliance are the republican elements of the financial aristocracy and the industrial bourgeoisie, with the support of the petty bourgeoisie.

There are other critical forces on the political stage – political forces to which no clear class designation corresponds, though their role and support is pivotal: the army, the press, the intellectual celebrities, the priests, the rural population. Occasionally, Marx hints at the class content of these supporting strata and coteries – for example, he calls the Mobile Guard 'the organised lumpen-proletariat'. This is the last moment when the Paris proletariat appears as a decisive actor; thereafter, the matter is settled 'behind the back of society'. But already it is in an alliance whose dominant fraction lies elsewhere. The republic thus reveals 'only the unrestricted despotism of one class over other classes'. This unstable political form then has, nevertheless, a structural and historical function: it is the classic 'political form for the revolutionising of bourgeois society'. Its 'history' in this moment is the short-lived 'history of the domination and dissolution of the republican fraction of the bourgeoisie'. Opposed to it is the 'Party of Order' – rallied behind the ancient slogans: property, family, religion, order. This alliance, in the conjuncture, appears in its double royalist disguise – Bourbon Legitimists and Orleanists. But this unstable bloc has its class composition too: behind the 'different shades of royalism' cluster 'big landed property', with *its* coterie and forces (priests and lackeys), and 'high finance, large-scale industry, large scale-trade, i.e. *capital*, with its retinue of advocates, professors and fine speech-makers'. Here, too, the struggle for predominance is masked by the need for unity in the face of the Party of Anarchy. What essentially divides them – driving each to 'restore its own supremacy and the subordination of the other interest' – is *not exclusively* their material conditions of existence ('two distinct sorts of property') but also the ideological traditions in which each has been formed. This is one of the many places where Marx demonstrates the pertinent, and the specific effectivity, of the *ideological* dimension of the class struggle upon the political, adding yet a further level of complexity: 'A whole superstructure of different and specifically formed interests and feelings, illusions, modes of thought and views of life arises on the basis of the different forms of property, of the social conditions of existence'. One must make, Marx adds, a sharp distinction 'between the phrases and fantasies of the parties and their real organisation and real interests, between their conceptions of themselves and what they really are'. In the conjuncture of May, what these fractions 'thought' of themselves, though referrable in the last instance to the material basis of their existence, had real and pertinent effects – as *The Eighteenth Brumaire* dramatically demonstrates. Marx performs the same kind of analysis – the formation of complex alliances, based on class fractions, their internal contradictions, the 'necessity' of the political positions, temporary programmes and ideological forms in which those 'interests' appear – for each 'moment' of the conjuncture of *Brumaire*.

The third point to note is the question of how these political fractions and strata achieve *political representation* in the course of the struggle. The two major fractions of the big bourgeoisie appear on the political stage in their respective royalist liveries: but the restoration of their respective ruling dynasties is not the objective 'work' which this alliance performs. Their union into and representation through the Party of Order brings on the question of the rule of the class 'as a whole', rather than the predominance of one fraction over another. Objectively, it is this temporary and unholy union which makes them the 'representatives of the bourgeois world order'. Time and again Marx returns to this central question of 'class content' and its *means of political representation*. It is not simply that the representation of class interests through political alliances and 'parties' is never a straightforward matter. It is also that the political interests of one class fraction can be represented through the role which another fraction plays on the political or the ideological stage. One excellent example is where Marx discusses the coalition of the proletariat and the petty-bourgeoisie into the 'so-called social democratic party'. This 'party' has its immediate determinations: it advances, temporarily, the interests of those left aside by the forceful regrouping of bourgeois forces. It has its contradictory internal structure: through their subordination within it the proletariat lose 'their revolutionary point' and gain 'a democratic twist'. Social democracy also has its objective *political* content:

'weakening the antagonism between capital and wage labour and transforming it into a harmony' (*MESW* (3), I, pp. 423–4. It is 'democratic' reform within the limits of bourgeois society.

It is in this precise context that Marx warns us about a too *reductive* conception of political representation. This temporary 'solution' is not petty-bourgeois because it advances the narrow interests of that transitional class. Its 'representatives' cannot be analysed in terms of the reduction to the narrow terms of their class designation – they are not all 'shopkeepers'. The *position* of this alliance is 'petty-bourgeois' in character because, temporarily, the *general* resolution to the crisis it proposes and endorses corresponds to the objective limits of the *particular* material interests and social situation of the petty bourgeois as a class. The political representatives, whoever they are and whatever their particular material designation, assume for the moment a petty-bourgeois political *position*, play a petty-bourgeois political role, propose a petty-bourgeois political resolution. It is the convergence, from different starting points, around these objective limits which – Marx argues – provides the basis for deciphering the 'general relationship between the political and literary representatives of a class and the class they represent' (*MESW* (3), I, p. 424). Thus, though the social and material limits and the objective class content set the terms and provide the horizon within which a 'petty-bourgeois' resolution to the crisis can appear, at a specific conjuncture, everything turns on the means and conditions which permit such a solution to surface and take a concrete shape as a *political force* in the theatre of the crisis.

It is this concept – of the *re-presentation* of the objective class content of the forces arrayed and the means and conditions of the political struggle, a struggle with its own forms of appearance, its own specific effectivity – which allows Marx to propose a dazzling solution to the central question which shadows *The Eighteenth Brumaire*. What does Napoleon, who does this exceptional suspension of the struggle through the execution of the coup d'état, *represent*? We know the solution for which Marx settled: he 'represents' the small-holding peasant – the conservative not the revolutionary peasant, the peasant who wants to consolidate, not the one who wants to strike out beyond the *status quo*.

We can only summarise in the barest outline how this 'solution' is constructed. It entails, first, an analysis of the specific mode of peasant production – based on the small holding – and of the form of social life which arises from it: the peasantry's isolation from mutual intercourse, its enforced self-sufficiency, the structure of village communities, its lack of diversity in development or wealth of social relationships. It traces the crucial transformation in the peasantry's economic role – from semi-serfdom into free landed proprietors – accomplished under the aegis of the first Napoleon. It relates the immediate consequences of this uneven transformation: the fragmentation of peasant property, the penetration of free competition and the market, the role in this backward and traditional sector of the money-lender, the mortgage and debt. Here the ravages of the disorganisation of peasant society by the capitalist invasion of the countryside is detailed. It is this which provides the basis of the developing antagonism between the peasantry and the bourgeoisie – an antagonism which gives Napoleon his 'independence'. Not only are the small-holding peasantry plunged into indebtedness; but the hidden burden of taxation fatally connects their immiseration with the swollen arms of the government and the executive apparatus of the state.

To this Marx adds a brilliant exposition of how the *ideological* outlook of the peasantry now finds, not a correspondence so much as a resonant *complementarity*, with the ideology of Louis Napoleon – 'Napoleon's ideas'. Napoleon's ideas are, in their objective content, nothing but 'the ideas of the undeveloped small holding in its heyday'. There is a 'homology of forms' between them. Does this mean that the Napoleonic solution has, after all, no correspondence with France's developing mode of production, no life-line to the bourgeoisie? It remains the fact, Marx suggests, that Napoleon can no longer directly represent any particular section of the bourgeoisie, for he has come to power only as the result of the successive defeat or retreat of each of its major fractions. This progressive liquidation founds the coup d'état on insecure and contradictory foundations. It is this which drives Napoleon to rest his political claims, finally, on a class which 'cannot represent themselves, they must be represented. Their representative must appear simultaneously as their master, as an authority over them, an unrestricted governmental power that protects them from the other classes and sends them rain and sunshine from above' (*MESW* (3), I, p. 479.) But it is just here – where a whole class fraction appears politically only through the exceptional political form of a one-man dictatorship –

that Marx executes the final ironic twist. For this makes the small-holding peasantry dependent, through Napoleon, directly on the executive – on *the state*.

It is in the maturing of state power, the creation of a swollen but 'independent' state machine, perfected through Napoleon's regime, and resting on the contradictory basis of his 'independence', that Bonaparte comes finally to do some service, not for this or that fraction of the bourgeoisie, but for the maturing of capitalist relations in France. 'The material interest of the French bourgeoisie is most intimately imbricated precisely with the maintenance of that extensive and highly ramified state machine. It is that machine which provides its surplus population with jobs, and makes up through state salaries for what it cannot pocket in the form of profits, interest, rent and fees. Its *political* interests equally compelled it daily to increase the repression, and therefore to increase the resources and personnel of state power. . . . 'The French bourgeoisie was thus compelled by its class position both to liquidate the conditions of existence of all parliamentary power, including its own, and to make its opponent, the executive, irresistible.' This is the long term 'work' which, through its reversals and detours, its advances and retreats, the 'crisis' of 1851 perfects and matures on behalf of the developing capitalist forces of French society. This is the objective labour which the revolution, performs 'on its journey through purgatory' (*MESW* (3), I, p. 476).

The level of the political class struggle, then, has its own efficacy, its own forms, its specific conditions of existence, its own momentum, tempo and direction, its own contradictions internal to it, its 'peculiar' outcomes and results. If everything is, here, governed in the last instance by the stage of development of the material and social relations through which the prevailing mode of production (and the subordinate or surviving modes of production which appear combined with it in any concrete society) reproduces itself, very little of the actual shifts in the political relations of class forces can be deciphered by reducing them back to the abstract terms of the 'principal contradiction'. The political *is* articulated with the level of the economic; and *both* (to make the distinction absolutely clear) are in a critical sense over-determined (constituted fundamentally by, and limited in the possible variants or outcomes) by the forces and relations combined within the 'mode of production'.

To suggest that they are not articulated, that there is no 'correspondence' of any kind, is to forfeit the first principle of historical materialism: the principle of social formations as a 'complex unity', as an 'ensemble of relations'. But that articulation is accomplished only through a series of displacements and disarticulations. Between the classes constituted in the economic relations of production, either in their 'pure' form (when the mode of production functions as an analytic framework) or in their concrete historical form (where they appear in complex forms, together with the formations of earlier modes) there intervenes a set of forms, processes, conditions and terms, graspable by a distinctive set of concepts – non-reducible concepts – which 'fill out' the level of the political in a social formation. The re-presentation of the 'economic' at the level of 'the political' must pass through these representational forms and processes. This is a process, a complex set of practices – the practices of the political class struggle: without them there would be no 'political' level at all. And once the class struggle is subject to the process of 'representation' in the theatre of political class struggle, that articulation is permanent: it obeys, as well as the determinations upon it, its own internal dynamic; it respects its own, distinctive and specific conditions of existence. It cannot be reversed. It is this transformation which produces and sustains the necessary level of appearance of the political. Once the class forces appear as political class forces, they have consequent political results; they generate 'solutions' – results, outcomes, consequences – which cannot be *translated back* into their original terms.

It is, of course, the 'raw materials' of the social relations of production – at the mode of production level – which provide the political class struggle with its elements. And the political results and conclusions 'won' or secured at the level of the political not only serve to articulate 'the political' as a permanent practice in any social formation – one which can *never* thereafter be an 'empty space' – they also have consequences for the manner in which the forces and relations of the material conditions of existence themselves develop. That is, they react, retrospectively, upon that which constitutes them – they have pertinent effects. The precise political form in which the 'compromise' of the 1851 coup d'état was struck is important both for the pace and for the character of capitalist development in France. It affects both the political and the economic life of French society. That 'reciprocal action' — if you like, of the political-ideological superstructures on the 'base' — does not operate in a 'free space'. Yet the precise direction and tendency of that reaction is not given exclusively by the forces and relations of the base: it is *also* given by the forces and relations of the political and the ideological struggle, and by all that is specific — relatively autonomous — to them. The superstructural results can 'react' upon the base by either favouring or hindering its development. Althusser noted that 'an over-determined contradiction may be either overdetermined in the direction of a historical inhibition, a real block . . . or in the direction of a revolutionary rupture, but in neither condition is it ever found in the "pure" state' (Althusser (1969), p. 106).

Engels, in his famous Letter to Schmidt, in which he dealt with this very question, suggested that:

The retroaction of the state power upon economic development can be one of three kinds: it can proceed in the same direction, and then things move more rapidly; it can move in the opposite direction . . . or it can prevent the economic development from proceeding along certain lines, and prescribe other lines (27 October 1890, *MESC*, p. 399).

This, Althusser comments, 'well suggests the character of the two limit positions' (Althusser (1969), p. 106, fn. 23). (It is important to note that this concept of 'determination' differs from the full-blown but more 'formal' notion of determination through 'structural causality' which Althusser and Balibar adopted for the exposition of *Reading Capital*. Its absence from the more formalist conception was one of the principal sources of the latter's 'theoreticist deviation'.)

Marx noted in the Introduction to the *Grundrisse* that, once we cease to think the relation between the different 'moments' of a process as *identical*, we are of necessity into the terrain of *articulation*. Articulation marks the forms of the relationship through which two processes, which remain distinct — obeying their own conditions of existence — are drawn together to form a 'complex unity'. This unity is therefore the result of 'many determinations', where the conditions of existence of the one does not coincide exactly with that of the other (politics to economic, circulation to production) *even if* the former is the 'determinate effect' of the latter; and that is because the former also have their own internal 'determinations'.

The concepts which Marx begins to elaborate and operate in *The Eighteenth Brumaire* – alliances, blocs, constitutional forms, regime, political representatives, political ideologies or 'ideas', fractions, factions, etc. – are the concepts which enable us to 'think' the complexity of this double determination. Since these political forms and relations are themselves constituted by the antagonistic class relations of the capitalist mode in which they appear, they are the concrete objects of the practices of class struggle – the class struggle in 'the theatre of politics'. The very term, 'theatre' and the sustained dramaturgical nature of Marx's style of exposition in the *Eighteenth Brumaire* underlines the *representational* aspect of this relation. This level is always present – it is always 'filled out' in one way or another – in any developed social formation. It performs a 'function' for the social formation as a whole, in that, at this instance there appears the forms and relations of the political through which the various fractions of capital and its political allies can contend, both among themselves and with the subordinate classes, so as to dominate the class struggle and to draw civil society, politics, ideology and the State into conformity with the broad underlying 'needs' of the developing mode of production. But those 'needs' never appear in their 'pure state'. Indeed, as Marx was obliged to observe in relation to Britain, the fundamental classes of capital never emerge full-blown and united and 'take charge of the social formation' in their own name and persona, 'for capital'. The distinction between the 'economically dominant class' and the 'politically leading or ruling caste', in Marx's and Engels's writings on Britain, recapitulates in miniature the distinctions, drawn *in extenso*, in *The Eighteenth Brumaire*, and provided the key to deciphering the class struggle in Britain: 'The governing caste . . . is by no means identical with the ruling class. . . .' ('Parties and Cliques' in *Surveys From Exile*, p. 279). The political level therefore also provides the necessary space of representation where those bargains, coalitions, 'unstable equilibria', are struck and dissolved which, *alone*, allow the 'laws of capital' to have pertinent effects.

It is consequently also in this 'space' – but also through its specific forms and relations – that the working class can struggle to contain the sway of capital in the form of its political representatives and forces, and, under a favourable conjuncture, to transform the *economic* structure of society by taking as its object the point where that structure is *condensed*: in the form of bourgeois state – i.e. *political* – power. It follows that we cannot conceive of 'the class struggle' as if classes were simply and homogeneously constituted at the level of the economic, and only then fractured at the level of the political. The political level is 'dependent' – determinate – because its 'raw materials' are given by the mode of production *as a whole*: a process of 'representation' must have something to represent. But classes are *complexly constituted* at each of the levels of the social formation – the economic, the political and the ideological. To grasp the 'state of play' in the relations of class forces in a concrete historical formation at a particular conjuncture *is* to grasp the necessary complexity and displacements of this 'unity'. It is only in the very exceptional conditions of a revolutionary rupture that the instances of these different levels will ever correspond. Thus to grasp the 'unity' of the class struggle, so constituted, is of necessity to grasp the question of classes *in its contradictory form*.

IV

Twenty years separate *The Eighteenth Brumaire* from *The Civil War in France*, in which Marx most directly extends some of the concepts elaborated in the former. It is a text whose conceptual developments are worked through directly in relation to a revolutionary political conjuncture requiring serious analysis (the Paris Commune), and is considerably influenced by Marx's and Engels's renewed political work in the context of the International (including the struggle against Bakunin and the Anarchists). Only three significant points can be indicated here from a body of political writing which is far too little studied and reflected upon in the Marxist movement.

The first concerns the indispensable necessity for the working class to constitute itself 'into a party': its aim being the 'conquest of the political power', its object, the rupture of the state and state power, 'the national power of capital over labour . . . a public force organised for social enslavement . . . an engine of class despotism'. In the Preface to the reissue of the *Manifesto* which Marx and Engels published in 1872, this 'lesson' was vividly enshrined: 'One thing especially was proved by the Commune, viz. that "the working class cannot simply lay hold of the ready-made state machinery and wield it for its own purpose".' The detailed analysis of the Commune not only constitutes Marx's most extended writing on the forms of proletarian political power, but contains the critical argument for what, in *The Critique of the Gotha Programme*, he calls 'a revolutionary dictatorship of the proletariat' as the only and necessary form in which the working class will 'have to pass through long struggles, through a series of historic processes, transforming circumstances and men' (*MESW*, pp. 327 and 291).

It is in this context that Marx returns to the question, already posed in *The Eighteenth Brumaire*, as to what class forces the figure and formation of the Napoleonic state represents, and the relation of the Napoleonic 'solution' to the economic development of capitalism in France. Here in *The Civil War in France* (*MESW*, pp. 285–6), Marx considerably elaborates on the growing autonomisation of the 'centralised power of the state'; he résumés the constitutional forms of the 1851 crisis through which this state power is matured and developed – the 'objective work' of the revolution; and the political work of domination over the under-developed fractions which they allowed Napoleon to accomplish. Here lies the basis for that theory of the state as a 'class state', of the state as the 'résumé of man's practical conflicts', the state as the relation of *political condensation*, which Lenin was subsequently to bring to a high order of importance (through his commentary on the fragmentary insights on this question of Marx and Engels in *State and Revolution*). One consequence of this emergent theory for our understanding of the relation between the political and economic aspects of the class struggle we will take up in a moment.

But first, Marx returns to the question of 'representation'. Napoleon, he now argues, 'professed to rest upon the peasantry, the large mass of producers not directly involved in the struggle of capital and labour' (*MESW* (3), II, p. 219). This class interest, apparently outside the direct play between the fundamental classes, served to substantiate the apparent 'autonomy' of Napoleon from the immediate terms of the struggle – it secured for his *coup* the appearance of autonomy. It thus enabled him to project his political intervention – a classic ideological function of the state – as incarnating the 'general interest', the 'representative' of all the classes (because it represented none), of 'the nation'. 'It professed to unite all classes by reviving for all the chimera of national glory' (ibid.).

Marx suggests how and why this form of political resolution related to the immediate relations of forces in the central arena of struggle – related to it, but *indirectly*, as a representation, *as a postponement of it.* 'In reality, it was the only form of government possible at a time when the bourgeoisie had already lost, and the working class had not yet acquired the faculty of ruling the nation' (ibid.). The 'postponement' of a political resolution – appearing in the political domain as the temporary but displaced 'rule' of an *absent* class – a class which could not appear in its own name – was a *form* which corresponded (but in no sense 'immediately') to the precise state of under-development of the class relations of capitalist production in France. But this 'unstable equilibrium', is also the condition which provides precisely the space through which the state drifts 'apparently soaring high above society' – incarnating but also at the same time *masking* the class struggle. And it is in this form – the form of 'the national power of capital over labour' (ibid.) – that capitalism in France *develops* – develops, of course, with its contradictory effects. Those effects are still to be seen in the peculiar form of 'étatisme' which capitalist development manifests in the French social formation. The demonstration could hardly be clearer of how powerful are the consequences of the political *for* the economic. Just as it could hardly be more evident that the political and the economic are *coupled* but not *as an identity relation.*

In this context, it is noteworthy that Marx returns to a passage in the *Manifesto* which we have previously discussed, and offers a clarification which is (in the light of *The Eighteenth Brumaire*) a necessary correction. In *The Critique of the Gotha Programme* Marx takes up Lassalle's misinterpretation of his assertion that, face to face with the working class, 'all other classes are a single reactionary mass' (i.e. the theses of the 'simplification of the classes' in political struggle). He makes two points of clarification. First, he reiterates that what made the bourgeoisie *the* revolutionary class *vis-à-vis* the feudal classes was its historic role as 'the bringer of large-scale industry'. It is this objective condition which also gives to the proletariat its revolutionary position. But this does not mean *collapsing* the other classes into a single mass. The remnants of feudal classes may play an objectively reactionary role, but 'these do not form a single reactionary mass together with the bourgeoisie' (*MESW* (3), III, p. 20). In short, the political analysis is now definitively identified as *requiring* a theory of the complex formation of class fractions in class alliances. These – not some indistinguishable fusion of whole classes – constitute the terms of the political class struggle.

Time and again, especially in the subsidiary writings of this period, both Marx and Engels return, on the basis of the theses of the International, to reaffirm the necessity of 'the political movement' as the means to the 'economical emancipation of the working class' (Speech on the Anniversary of the International, Fernbach (1973–4), *The First International and After*, p. 271). The more the theory of the state and the centrality of state power to the expansion of capitalism is developed, the more central becomes the role of the political struggle at the forefront of 'the social revolution'. It is true, as Fernbach observes, that Marx and Engels never work their way through to a fully developed theory of the corporate forms of working-class economic and political struggle: and he is right to attribute their failure, on the whole, to grasp the nature of the working class movement in Britain to this theoretical lacuna (Fernbach (1973), *Surveys from Exile*, pp. 22–4). One has to turn to Lenin's polemic against Martynov and the 'economists' for an adequate theorisation of this tendency. This debate cannot be presented here; but the whole Chapter on 'Trade Union Politics and Social-Democratic Politics', in Lenin's *What Is To Be Done?*, needs to be read in the context of this question: for the confusions which Lenin confronts there remain to plague us, with greatly augmented force, today (Lenin, *CW*, vol. 5, pp. 397–440). The view that, because the economic relations and foundations determine, in the last instance, the forms and outcomes of the class struggle, therefore the struggle *waged at the level of the economic* is (as Martynov declared) 'the most widely applicable method' of struggle, is dismantled by Lenin with all the cogency of his polemical force. He calls the proposition 'the quintessence of Economism'; and this designation leads him into an analysis of the corporate character of a struggle limited to the battle 'for better terms in the sale of their labour power, for better conditions of life and labour', which takes us, in turn, directly to the heart of social-democratic reformism and 'economism' – to 'the soundly scientific (and "soundly" opportunist) Mr and Mrs Webb and . . . the British Trade unions' (*What Is To Be Done? CW*, vol. 5, p. 404). What Lenin's intervention (and its subsequent development in the setting of his theory of imperialism) brings out far more sharply than Marx does, is the *damage* which has been wrought by the use, by Marx and by Marxists after him, of the same *term* – the 'economic' – to designate *two* quite different things: the relations and forces of the mode of production and the site of those practices and forms of struggle which have economic relations (e.g. conditions of work, or wages) as their specific object.

V

We can conclude by attempting very briefly to say how we begin to understand these terms and their effect for the constitution of classes and the class struggle. The 'master concept' is that of mode of production. 'Mode of production' is, in the first instance, the conceptual or analytic matrix which allows us to think, systematically, the fundamental structures of relations by means of which men, under determinant historical conditions, produce and reproduce the material conditions of their life. It consists of 'forces' and 'relations' – but this is only a summary formulation. Grasped within these apparently simple terms are sets of relations: relations both between agents and instruments, and agents and agents of production: the technical and the social division of labour under developing capitalist conditions – in which Marx gives priority of position to the 'social' over the 'technical'. But even the 'social' relations are not simple: they relate both to ownership of the means, organisation of the actual labour process and the power to set men and means, in certain combinations, to work.

The brief résumé we have offered of the 'Machinery and Modern Industry' chapter from *Capital* should be enough to suggest how different sets of relations, in combination, are indexed by the ready formula of 'forces and relations'. To this we would have to add the 'corresponding relations' of circulation and exchange – which are necessary to complete the long circuit of capital's realisation. When we say that the term, 'mode of production' is, first, an analytic matrix, we mean simply that it gives us a concept of the terms and the relations – the places and the conditions which must be filled – for what we can recognise as 'production under capitalist conditions' to take place. It designates the fundamental places and spaces into which agents and means of production must be distributed, and where they are combined for capitalist production to proceed. It fundamentally designates the *site* of *class* relations in the economic structure of capitalism, since each of those positions entails antagonistic relations – antagonisms which Marx constantly invokes in his analysis in *Capital* through the 'personifications', capitalist and wage-labourer. The site of classes does not designate 'whole' classes as integral empirical groups of men and women; rather it indicates functions. As any sophisticated analysis of the anatomy of classes under the different phases of capitalist development clearly indicates, classes can shift at least some of their positions in relation to these functions: or they can perform 'functions' on, so to speak, either side of the line of class antagonism.

This analysis is of particular importance in the designation of, for example, the new middle classes, which perform some (but not all) of the functions of *both* 'global capital' *and* 'the collective worker' (to use Carchedi's terms, as illustration, for the moment (Carchedi, 1975). Thus in the actual concrete functioning of a particular mode of production, at any particular phase of its development, in a concrete historical society or social formation, the constitution of classes at this 'economic' level is *already* complex and, in certain critical respects, contradictory. The idea that, somehow, by employing the terms of 'mode of production' we can produce empirically-constituted 'whole classes' at the level of the economic, is an untenable proposition.

There are two, additional, reasons why this must be so. First, in actual concrete, historic, social formations, modes of production do not appear in their 'pure' state, on their own. They are always combined with, and stand in a complex articulation to, other, previous or subordinate, modes of production – and their corresponding political and ideological relations – which cross-cut and over-determine any tendency of 'pure' mode to produce a series of 'pure' classes.

The second reason has already been anticipated. Social formations do not consist of an articulation of modes of production alone, but always sustain superstructural relations – the political, the juridical, the ideological. And, because these are not the mere efflorescences of the 'base', they have pertinent effects: they have an effect of further complexifying the constitution of classes. Indeed, they exert an over-determining effect in two, different ways. First, the political, juridical and ideological have effects *within* what we have broadly designated as 'the economic'. In certain phases of capitalist development, the real and the juridical ownership of the means of production coincides. But in, for example, monopoly capitalist conditions, the two functions do *not* coincide. Corporate property may be partly 'owned' juridically by social groups who do not possess the 'real' power to set the instruments of that property to work in production. But the political, juridical and the ideological also have *their own* effects, just as they have their own, determinate, conditions of existence, not reducible to 'the economic'. And since, as we have tried to demonstrate, these are related but 'relatively autonomous' practices, and thus the sites of distinct forms of class struggle, with their own objects of struggle, and exhibiting a relatively independent retroactive effect on 'the base', the forms in which classes, class interests and class forces *appear*, at each of these levels, will by no means necessarily fall in the same place, or indeed correspond in their form with that of another level. The example of the peasantry, Napoleon, the stalemate between the fundamental classes, the expansion of the state and capital, in *The Eighteenth Brumaire* should be enough to convince us of the non-immediacy, the non-transferability between these levels. The 'general' concept of classes and of the class struggle, in its different aspects, will consist of our ability to grasp the *global* effect of these complex, contradictory effects. This implies a non-homogeneous conception of classes − including, for example, the non-homogeneity of capital, shorthand for the different kinds of capital, whose internal composition and differences of position in the circuit ensures that it has no singular, unproblematic 'interest', even at the level of the economic. Hence it is most unlikely to appear as an integral force on the political stage, not to speak of the impossibility of conceiving it as appearing at the level of the ideological having, so to speak, 'made up *its* mind'.

In the foregoing sections we have been trying to explore just how Marx arrived at, and then how conceptually he filled out, the terms of this 'non-homogeneity'. Just to make the point a practical one, we need to think only of the significance of the moments in recent European history when 'capital' has appeared to exert its compelling force ideologically, putting on the mask or draping itself in the robes (to use two metaphors from *The Eighteenth Brumaire*) of the petty-bourgeoisie (the class which, to coin a phrase, has nothing to lose but its moral rectitude).

These ideological displacements and disguisings are by no means confined to the past. One could read the economic and political situation in Britain since the early 1960s as a deepening crisis of the economic structure which assumes its most 'natural' expression, at the political level, in the form of a Labour government – a paradoxical situation, where, in crisis, the party most favoured by capital is the 'representative party of the working class'. But this may have a great deal to do with what that party does when in power: living up, almost to the letter, to the description, offered in *The Eighteenth Brumaire*, of one of the historic roles of Social Democracy – 'as a means not of doing away with two extremes, capital and wage-labour, but as weakening their antagonism and transforming it into harmony' (*The Eighteenth Brumaire*, *MESW* (3), I, pp. 423–24.). When Social Democracy attempts both to serve capital and represent the working class, it frequently does this by raising the index of its power to that of the 'general interest': an interest which then, ideologically, appears in the rhetoric of Social Democracy in the ideological personification of 'the consumer'. On the other side of the parliamentary scene, we can observe the Thatcher leadership preparing for power and constructing an authoritarian popular consensus, in part by attempting to 'represent' capital (anachronistically, but no less effectively) in the 'venerable disguise and borrowed language', the 'names, slogans and costumes' of a disappearing class fraction – the small shopkeeper! There could hardly be a more compelling argument – to anyone seeking to unravel the thread of class struggle which unites these discrepant appearances – for a theory of class struggle *as* a theory of the 'unity' of these contradictory and displaced representations of class relations at a series of different sites or instances – the economic; the political; the ideological. In short, the need for a Marxist theory of representation, of *Darstellung*.

In the context of the debate about ideology, this concept of 're-presentation' has been recently much criticised by Hirst (Hirst (1976)) as being no more than a complex version of a 'reflection' theory, with a tendency to return to the 'givenness of the classes as social forces in the structure of the economic' (ultimately economistic) and a reliance on what he calls the 'base-superstructure contestation', which he defines as tending 'towards vulgar materialism'. This argument is conducted against, especially, Althusser's theory of ideology, as developed in the article on 'ideological state apparatuses' (Althusser (1971)), and therefore poses problems of an order outside the immediate framework of this essay. However, Hirst goes on to criticise the very concept of 'representation' suggesting that if 'representation' is used in its strong form, then the means by which relations are represented absolutely transform them; hence those means determine the form of 'representation', which can then never be re-examined in terms of what is 'represented'. 'It is not too much to argue that once any autonomy is conceded to these means of representation, it follows necessarily that the means of representation determine the represented. This obliterates the classic problem of "representation"' (Hirst, p. 395).

This argument appears to take the thesis concerning the non-transferability, the non-homogeneity, of the economic and political levels of class struggle (which we have been trying to establish in terms of its reference points in Marx's own work) to its *opposite extreme*, in the effort to banish every last strain of reductionism from the Marxist schema. From this position there follows what Hirst has been bold enough to name the 'necessary non-correspondence' of the levels – a concept very different in fact from that of *'no necessary correspondence'*. The difference between the two seems to me to be, precisely, the difference between *autonomy* and *relative autonomy*. And whereas 'relative autonomy' appears, from the texts we have been examining, to catch exactly the way Marx sets out to think the *complex unity* of a social formation (both *complexity* and *unity* having equal importance), autonomy, or a 'necessary non-correspondence' appears to fall outside the limits of Marxism as an identifiable theoretical terrain. It seems clear, from the passages I have examined, that Marx *does* advance to a concept of non-correspondence, not in any simple, reductionist or homogeneous sense: he develops the concepts which enable us to think, in relation to specific historical conjunctures, just *how* and why these displacements have effects; what forms and relations sustain them in their 'relative' independence; and what effects and consequences the non-reducibility of the structure of a social formation to its 'base' has for the understanding and the continuation of class struggle as a complex practice. It seems equally clear that Marx *does* – as Althusser has now openly recognised (Althusser (1976)) – continue to think the economic structure as in some sense other than a reductionist one, 'determining': that this does require the – quite new and original – problem of grasping a 'unity' which is *not* a simple or reductionist one: that it is precisely this double movement which constitutes *The Eighteenth Brumaire* as the most remarkable of Marx's non-reductionist materialist analyses of politics: and that this conception does, finally, require the Marxist 'topography' of base and superstructure. Indeed, what the base-superstructure topography 'does' for Marxism, and why it provides a defining conceptual threshold and boundary-limit *for* Marxism (without which it becomes another thing, another kind of theory – a theory of the absolute autonomy of everything from everything else) is most eloquently expressed in Althusser's *Essays in Self-Criticism*: all the more pertinent in this case since it was his acknowledged 'theoreticist deviation' which prompted, in the name of Marxism, a rigorous and often highly principled tendency to depart from its terrain. In the light of this continuing debate, therefore, it seemed worthwhile undertaking an investigation of how Marx himself made the theoretical departure from the terrain of essentialism and simplicity, and how, in detail, the concepts were forced into discovery which enabled him – and us, after him – to grasp the radical and necessary complexity of the practice of class struggle.

REFERENCES AND ABBREVIATIONS

Althusser, 1969, *For Marx*, Allen Lane (London, 1969).

Althusser, 1971, 'Ideology and the Ideological State Apparatuses' in *Lenin and Philosophy and Other Essays*, New Left Books (London, 1971).

Althusser, 1976, *Essays in Self-Criticism*, New Left Books (London, 1976).

Carchedi, 1975, 'On the Economic Identification of the New Middle Class', *Economy and Society*, no. 4, pp. 1–86.

Fernbach, 1973–4, Introductions to Marx, *The Revolutions of 1848; Surveys from Exile* and *The First International and After*, Penguin (Harmondsworth, 1973, 1974).

Gramsci, 1971, *Prison Notebooks*, Lawrence and Wishart (London, 1971).

Hirst, 1976, 'Althusser and the Theory of Ideology', *Economy and Society*, no. 5, pp. 385–412 (1976).

Lenin, *CW*, *Collected Works* (45 vols), Lawrence and Wishart (London, 1960–70).

Lukács, *History and Class Consciousness*, Merlin Press (London, 1971).

MECW, *Marx–Engels Collected Works*, Lawrence and Wishart (London, 1975ff).

MESW (1) *Marx–Engels Selected Works* (in one volume), Lawrence and Wishart (London, 1970).

MESW (3), *Marx–Engels Selected Works* (in 3 volumes), Progress (Moscow, 1969–1970).

MESC, *Marx–Engels Selected Correspondence*, Progress (Moscow, 1975).

German Ideology, Marx and Engels, *The German Ideology*, Lawrence and Wishart, (London, 1965).

Capital I, Marx, *Capital* I, Lawrence and Wishart (London, 1970).

Capital III, Marx, *Capital* III, Lawrence and Wishart (London, 1972).

Civil War, Marx, *The Civil War in France, MESW* (1 vol.), Lawrence and Wishart (London, 1970).

Gotha Programme, Marx, *Critique of the Gotha Programme, MESW* (1 vol.).

Eighteenth Brumaire, Marx, *The Eighteenth Brumaire of Louis Bonaparte, MESW* (3 vols.).

Poverty of Philosophy, Marx, *The Poverty of Philosophy, MECW*, vol. 6, pp. 105–212.

Communist Manifesto, Marx and Engels, *The Manifesto of the Communist Party, MESW* (1 vol.) pp. 35–63; and *The Revolutions of 1848*, Penguin (Harmondsworth, 1973).

Grundrisse, Marx, *Grundrisse*, Penguin (Harmondsworth, 1973).

Poulantzas, 1973, *Political Power and Social Classes*, New Left Books (London, 1973).

Williams, 1976, *France 1848–1851*, Open University (A321, Units 5–8).

THE DIFFERENTIATION OF
THE WORKING CLASS

Vic Allen

I. BOURGEOIS CATEGORIES

The issue before me, posed by the title of the paper, concerns the composition of the working class. What, in the first instance, is the meaning of the term 'working class'? How does it relate to other contiguous classes, if such classes exist? Who are to be excluded from the working class and for what reasons? And what is the significance of inclusion or exclusion for understanding the social behaviour of groups in particular and social movements in general. The questions are important ones.

In the main, the question of differentiation amongst people in contemporary capitalist societies has been treated in class terms but without any agreement about the meaning of class. Indeed class is one of the most confused and confusing of major sociological terms. The prevalent conventional analysis of differentiation has emphasised social class as the main distinguishing characteristic and has elaborated multiple class structures. Populations have been distributed between social classes in which it is assumed there is a common identity, a sense of belonging and the prospect, therefore, of common responses to various pressures. The multiple structure has been intended to show that universal pressures would produce differentiated, contrasting responses. In other words, class has been used to denote those people holding a common position along some continuum of the society.

A very large difficulty in the way of analysing class and class composition is the existence and pervasiveness of conventional sociological categories which represent a particular protective model of society. For the majority of sociologists multiple class structures are taken as given. The only questions are what is meant by multiplicity, that is, how many social class categories are there? and what labels should be pinned on each of the categories? In conventional sociological theory class differentiation is taken to mean stratification. All social class analysis, then, is about the character of stratification and not whether or not stratification exists. The omission is important because stratification carries with it three implications which encourage an acceptance of the capitalist system. Firstly stratification implies a hierarchical distribution of classes in a ranked order so that some classes are superior or inferior to others. Secondly it implies that each layer is smaller than the one below it; that society has a social class pyramidal shape with a base and an apex. Thirdly, it implies that social status increases from the base to the apex so that the largest class has the lowest social status and the smallest has the highest social status. In effect, this form of analysis is a legitimation of an elitist society. It leaves unquestioned the elitist character and fills in with largely irrelevant detail.

Conventional social class theory works for the system and despite its sophisticated approach it is essentially the same as the eighteenth- and early nineteenth-century classification when workers were described as the 'labouring poor' or the 'lower orders' in contrast to the 'gentry' or their 'betters.'[1] The location of workers in the class structure was attributed largely to personality defects thus becoming a question of individualism. At one and the same time the 'lower orders' were exhorted to accept the inevitability of their ranking and reminded that only through their individual qualities could they escape into the higher status classes. The contemporary stratified model is projected as an aspirational pattern for those who commit themselves to the dominant values of the system, work hard and are thrifty. Movement, meaning progress, through the social class categories is regarded as an individual matter, depending upon exercising those qualities most likely to consolidate the *status quo*.

Social class analysis which stipulates a working class with its own built-in divisions such as unskilled, semi-skilled and skilled groups or, as in the work of Lockwood and Goldthorpe,[2] traditional, deferential and privatised groups, and which break down contiguous classes into lower middle, middle and upper-middle in a distinctly pyramidal form, is primarily of ideological significance. It is static and descriptive. It places populations into social class positions and then attributes consequences to them, such as demographic rates, various pathologies, voting behaviour, criminal tendencies, racial, religious and sex attitudes. Thus it imposes a predetermined model on the population and distributes data in a manner which confirms the categories stipulated in the model. Moreover, its categories are entirely derived from white male data for it is assumed that the class position of women is determined by that of men in their kinship groups and that society possesses an ethnic homogeneity.

It may be the case that conventional social class categories are the figments of sociologists' imagination for they are made within the static framework of empiricism in which causality is anyone's guess. Choose a variable and it is as good as any other. However, every variable represents some distinction while some, such as income, education and life-style are sufficiently plausible to go unquestioned· as class-differentiating ones. These distinctions, not in spite of their superficiality but because of it, have entered through the dominant paradigm into common, everyday usage. People in general use the social class terms of sociologists and, when requested, posit themselves in one or other of them. By reference to a few indices such as income, job status, education, status of father, people can quickly pigeon-hole themselves. Indeed, the conventional categories have become so commonplace that answers to 'which class are you in?' tend to be answered as if through intuition. All of this reinforces the initial model of stratification with all its implications.

The important thing to remember about conventional social class analysis is that it is not analysis at all but descriptive and classificatory. Because it concentrates on visible phenomena and ignores hidden structural determinants it can say nothing about causes. It cannot, therefore, account for changes in any of its own class categories. It can tabulate. The working class is getting smaller and the lower middle class is getting bigger, for example. It can specify the occupational groups which might be represented in one class or other. It cannot account for changes between and within occupational groups and in any case it is interested in such groups only in so far as they relate to income, education and life-style variables.

II. THE CONCRETE REALITY OF CAPITALISM

An effective analysis of class formation must, in the first instance, start without a presupposition about its existence and its form. In the second instance, it must relate to aspects of behaviour which are vital for the system. In this respect I agree with Nicos Poulantzas who states that 'Classes exist only in the class struggle,'[3] though what precisely constitutes 'class struggle' is a question which may divide us. As no one is exempt from the 'class struggle,' that is from taking sides in the issue concerning the protection or alteration of the system, class formation must be about relative positions in that struggle. Classes, if they exist, must represent different institutional perceptions of relations with the existing order. They cannot simply comprise individual perceptions with no unifying elements. Class analysis based in the concrete reality of capitalism should tell us about the formation and distribution of political allegiances not simply through voting patterns but through an identification with policies about everyday affairs. It should inform us about the distinction between the professed intentions of individuals and class action. It should identify the contradictions which may exist within classes, for instance concerning racism and sexism. And it should reveal the contradictions which may act on classes to alter their composition and to determine their experience. Class analysis must be about the distribution and utilisation of power.

The starting point of the analysis must be the concrete reality of capitalism. We start, therefore, with social relations of production and the prime division between the owners and non-owners of the means of production, or the buyers and sellers of labour power which it embodies. If our analysis is to be logically consistent with the assumption that the social relations of production comprise the structure of a system, then the manner in which that structure penetrates the experience of everyday life must be the prime determinant of those experiences. The social relations of production in a capitalist society do not simply create the existence of a market relationship between those who are compelled to sell their labour power for subsistence and the owners of the means of production; they involve a process of exploiting labour power in order to extract surplus value. The market relationship and the process of exploitation are part of the same totality. The market relationship separates the worker from his labour power. It is labour power which is hired out or sold into the control of the owners of the means of production and manipulated through pressure on either its cost or its skill in order to maximise profits. The dynamic in this process of exploitation is derived from the contradiction between relations of production and the forces of production which creates intensive, perpetual, irresolvable market pressures on employers. The core of the reality of the prime structural contradiction is the experience of sellers of labour power at the point of production. The social relations of production, of course, permeate the totality of life experiences, with those outside of the point of production simply confirming those within it. Nothing that happens apart from the work situation can be autonomous of or superior to that which happens in it. In the reality of everyday experiences there are no prime, secondary and internal contradictions. These are analytical categories. There are simply contradictions. These contradictions act within the labour process. The question has to be asked whether they create divisions between sellers of labour power which produce contrasting, inconsistent responses to uniform pressures. If they do, then possibly the divisions represent class boundaries between sellers of labour power.

What I am saying, in effect, is that class divisions of any and every kind must be of the same order of causal magnitude as that embodied in the social relations of production. There is no logic, and therefore, no theoretical credibility in *ad hoc* theorising such as would be involved in emphasising the social relations of production and rejecting its divisive implications for everyday life. It can be said, moreover, that if contradictions do not create recognisably contrasting forms of behaviour amongst the sellers of labour power then there are no significant class divisions between them. The next step in the analysis is an examination of the exigencies involved in selling labour power in order to establish whether or not sellers constitute a class and, if so, of what order.

III. A CLASS OF SELLERS

Those who sell their labour power have certain characteristics in common. They all, as individuals, have a relationship of inferiority with employers. There is no exception to this. There are many sellers and few buyers in all markets for labour power giving the balance of power to the buyers. A buyer of labour power can choose and discriminate between sellers; he can dispense with labour power and, because of his proprietary control over it, he can manipulate and dilute its skill in relation to other sellers or to machines.

Labour power is obtained for its skill content and there are wide variations in its provision from individuals. The greater the specificity of the skill the greater the power the person who provides it in relation to an employer. But specificity is a two-edged thing. It hampers the short-run ability of an employer to get a replacement but it also restricts the manœuverability of the seller. On balance, however, the seller has the advantage from skill specificity but he never loses his power inferiority. An employer can always dilute specific skills by mechanising them in part or total.

Sellers of labour power, too, work in order to live. The whole point of working is to earn incomes not to produce commodities or to engage in particular production processes. This is common to all sellers of labour power. Quite clearly some sellers are able to have a greater interest in the commodities they produce than others, and some have a greater and more obvious attachment to production processes than others. But no sellers can ignore the imperative need to subsist if their skills are discarded. People of all income levels and status are compelled to cart their skills around in varying forms when confronted by unemployment.

There is no doubt that selling labour power possesses common objectives which can be characterised by inferiority, helplessness, subordination, subjugation to varying extents and that these elements are sufficiently important as determinants of behaviour to constitute a common objective economic position. This is so despite the differences in the level of income, authority, status and life-style of sellers of labour power. It was the recognition of this fact which led Marx to talk about two classes, one for the buyers and one for the sellers, which existed irrespective of the perceptions of those involved. Sellers of labour power belong to a 'class in itself'.

The question at issue here is whether all members of a labour market who sell labour power, despite their skills and status and involvement in the production process, can be located in the same objective economic position. Might it not be, as Poulantzas suggests, that some adopt class positions, or stances and are not in a class which is determined for them.[4] Might not some sellers vacillate between classes as circumstances vary and belong to neither? Might not certain categories of sellers really take the place of the small, independent shop-keepers and artisans as the *petty bourgeoisie*. and, therefore, stand midway between the working class and the bourgeoisie? Nicos Poulantzas who contends this is so will doubtless argue his own case. Here, I am concerned only with my own argument.

Three questions arise at this juncture. Firstly what is the occupational composition of the sellers of labour power and how do they compare or contrast with each other? Secondly what changes are occurring — what is new about the composition — and of what significance are they? Thirdly what evidence is there of common responses and what does it indicate?

IV. IDEOLOGICALLY DETERMINED LABOUR MARKETS

The historical development of production has evolved through the continual application of the division of labour between occupations and within them so that the sellers of labour power have been distributed among a multiplicity of skills involved in an even greater multiplicity of tasks. It is the totality of this which comprises the labour process. Each of the occupations and its sub-divisions has its own skill requirements, its own status and its own price. There is no direct correlation between skills, as technical competence, status and price, for what is a skill is ideologically determined.

There is no way at this level of analysis whereby the economic can be separated from the ideological, for ideology has material consequences as real as any others in and around the work situation. Tasks which have an ideological ranking tend to provide monetary and non-monetary rewards in the same order. Workers in high status jobs tend to have higher earnings, shorter and more cogenially distributed working hours, better working conditions, longer holidays and more social amenities in general than those in jobs ranked below them. These distinctions spill over into educational and job opportunities and life-styles in general and tend, therefore, to be reinforced by them.

This ideological dispersion of skills covers every aspect of work. It is not simply concerned with distinguishing between manual and non-manual. There is no task in the whole process of production, exchange and distribution which is not ranked according to its usefulness to the system in spite of and often contrary to its own objective skill qualities. This ranking is legitimised by complex prescriptions concerning job qualifications, the length and intensity of training, the nature of training, which all fit in neatly with the elitist character of the system. We accept the ranking because it is part, an essential part, of the dominant paradigm. When we think of work we think of the categories, unskilled, semi-skilled, skilled, clerical, administrative, executive and professional, and we use the value-loaded terms, jobs, occupations and professions to designate them.

A consequence of what can be called the institutionalised perception of work is the creation of socially determined labour markets between which there is restricted mobility. These labour markets comprise jobs with comparable ideologically determined skills, possessing similar prescriptions for recruitment and training. They possess an insularity which creates contradictions amongst the sellers of labour power and leads to problems of class definition.

I am suggesting that in order to get an insight into the composition of class forces we should examine the labour process within socially determined labour markets and analyse the relationships between and within them. If all sellers of labour power belonged to a single, homogeneous labour market there would be competition between individuals who were subjected to similar experiences. The would not be divided by contradictions. We could assume that they would have similar perceptions of themselves in relation to employers and the system. The reality of sellers, however, is not like this. They belong to different but related labour markets with institutionalised means of self-preservation. The labour markets stand in different relationships with each other, to employers and, therefore, to the capitalist system. But they operate within a context of economic pressures which shows no regard for their distinguishing features. The main pressures come from changes in the level of employment and technological change. Both of these break down exclusiveness and equalise experiences. In doing so they penetrate and alter institutionalised perceptions of work.

I need to emphasise that just as the act of selling labour power is more than a market transaction in that it implies a process of extracting surplus value, so it is with socially determined labour markets. Within each labour market there are common labour processes but between them they vary. What I have done, in effect, is to move from a consideration of individual sellers of labour power to that of institutionalised sellers. Through the empirical identification of these labour markets it is possible to see the imposition of distinctions on to a common objective economic position. Contradictions from within the capitalist mode of production alter demarcation lines between jobs, tasks, occupations, whichever term is preferred, through lowering, abolishing or raising their skill content or by changing materials. They impose divisions between groups of workers and create friction between them. The unity between the sellers of labour power in very restricted industrial groupings is continually impaired in this way. All contiguously related institutionalised work activities can be altered in their relationships in this way. The ideological dispersion of skills groups contiguous work activities into labour markets with generally common sources of recruitment, training and control. Thus it adds another dimension to the contradictions by intensifying the insularity of particular groups of workers, inhibiting mobility between types of work represented by the labour markets and by obtaining the acceptance of the divisions by workers themselves.

In other words, in general, the aspirations of workers are contained or limited by the scope of the respective labour markets.

This analytical model has particular advantages. First it does not demarcate artificially because whatever lines of demarcation separate the sellers of labour power from each other have to be established empirically. This is especially important because there is a tendency to make analytical distinctions which, whilst they may fit logically into a model, are not real to people. It is not necessary, of course, for the distinctions to be apparent or visible but real in the sense that they represent separate modes of behaviour.

Secondly, it does not prejudge the issue by specifying beforehand what the distinctions are, as in the case of the acceptance of manual and non-manual categories. This particular distinction may indeed be important in certain instances but its relevance has to be a question, leaving open the possibility that it might have no significance at all.

Thirdly, the model involves no hierarchy and, therefore, no ranking order. All it implies is that there are likely to be different institutionalised perceptions of relationships with employers and different degrees and forms of involvement in the class struggle from and within one ideologically determined labour market to another. It rejects, therefore, the notion of social class or social stratum for distinguishing between sellers of labour power.

Fourthly, there is no presumption that ideologically determined labour markets are homogeneous so that all that has to be analysed are the relationships between them. The intention of demarcating workers is to enable the forces acting on them to be analysed more effectively so that we can see precisely what determines their experiences. We want to know about the contradictions in the consciousness of particular workers. What is it, for example, that produces racism of an extreme kind in dockers and meat porters in London? What is the incidence and cause of sexism amongst workers?

Fifthly and lastly, no hard and fast lines are drawn between sellers of labour power. The main lines in the model are ideological and these are susceptible to pressures for change. The historical development of the labour force in Britain during the nineteenth and twentieth centuries is proof of this. The general ideological emphasis to tailor people's aspirations to suit the requirements of a capitalist system has remained unaltered. But the pattern of its emphasis, what it sanctions and what it does not sanction, has changed because the survival needs of the system have themselves changed.

V. THE COMPOSITION OF THE LABOUR FORCE

Many profound changes have occurred in capitalist societies through their competitive struggles with each other and with the expanding Socialist sector of the world. Methods of production have altered and the pace of technological change has quickened; production has been concentrated in increasingly larger units; the degree of monopoly has also increased, spreading through multi-national companies over national boundaries. No capitalist countries have been exempted from the changes but each has had its own unique experiences, depending largely upon its historical position in the development of capitalism. Britain from its position as the first major capitalist country has gone through more changes than most to become what can now be described as a satellite to the dominant capitalist countries, the USA, West Germany and Japan.

In the process of adapting to and coping with changes in international capitalism the composition of the British labour force and the relations between its parts, have continually changed. In the early development of British capitalism the labour force was essentially an apprentice-skilled one, due to the sixteenth century Statute of Apprentices, with a fringe of casual labour, concentrated in the large towns. Under the impact of simple mechanised processes crafts were split, creating new ones, and then diluted. The act of dilution created tasks which could be tackled without apprentice training. At the same time new industries, coal mining and iron production developed outside of the jurisdiction of the Statute of Apprentices, employing people whose skills were obtained from experience. Many of these non-apprentice skilled workers performed tasks which were no less skilled in terms of technical competence than those undertaken by craftsmen but they were designated as semi-skilled or unskilled. This was the case in the iron and steel industry where all production work involving a high level of technical competence was done by semi-skilled workers and where craftsmen performed only maintenance jobs. The distinction between craftsmen and others, however, during the period of extensive dilution from 1850 to 1900, was not simply about who was and who was not skilled; it represented a social difference which was reflected in the attempts of craftsmen to be exclusive, to reject unity with lesser skilled, even to castigate them for their lack of social graces, inferior education and profligate habits. But there is no question that the displacement of the educated elite in the labour force by the relatively uneducated without craft-skills, significantly altered the perception and involvement of workers in the class struggle.

Other changes were occurring simultaneously with the dilution of craft-skills. There was the movement of workers from agriculture to manufacturing and primary industry. Between 1851 and 1901 the proportion of workers in civilian employment engaged in agriculture in Britain fell from 22·06 per cent to 9·05 per cent. This proportion was as low as 1·55 in 1970. The decline of agriculture in both absolute and relative terms resulted in a labour force which was both concentrated in designated semi-skilled and unskilled jobs in factories and urbanised. This transition moved workers between different ideologically determined labour markets from one still influenced by feudal conceptions of social relationships to one in which class divisions were recognised. This phenomenon was common to all capitalist countries though it occurred at different periods with different rates of intensity.

The expansion of the size of production units and the increase in the degree of monopoly accentuated the growth of administration within firms and as servicing agents for productive industry. Monopoly problems caused entrepreneurs to concentrate on selling rather than producing with the consequent increase in sales organisations. At the same time, management and supervisory tasks multiplied and a hierarchy of management control was established. As the productive capacity of industry got greater so did the service industries increase in number and expand in size. The result was a redistribution of labour between agriculture, fishing and forestry as a group, manufacturing industry and the service industries. The table below shows the extent of this redistribution. The proportion of the civilian labour force employed in manufacturing remained remarkably cons ant. In 1841 it

GREAT BRITAIN

Percentage distribution of the numbers in civilian employment by sector, 1841–1970

Year*	Agriculture, Forestry and Fishing	Manufacturing	Services and Administration
1841	22·44	35·80	27·64
1851	22·06	38·80	27·19
1861	19·05	39·07	30·52
1871	15·63	37·38	32·70
1881	13·43	36·97	35·84
1891	10·83	37·38	38·55
1901	9·05	38·02	40·73
1911	8·57	38·93	41·85
1921	7·57	30·16	40·60
1931	6·68	26·06	53·83
1941	5·53	41·67	41·72
1951	5·78	27·07	56·04
1961	4·13	26·74	55·21
1970†	1·55	36·01	47·66

* 1841–1921 based on 1911 census; 1931 and 1951 based on 1951 census.
† Excluding employers and self employed (Source D.E.P. Gazette, March 1971).

Source: British Labour Statistics, Historical Abstract 1886–1968. Tables 102, 103, 104, 105, 116.

was 35·8 per cent and in 1970, 36·01 per cent. Fluctuations in between had been induced by cylical swings in trade and employment. The proportion employed in services and administration, on the other hand had increased from 27·64 per cent in 1841 to 40·73 per cent in 1901. It rose to 55·21 per cent in 1961 and then fell to 47·66 per cent in 1970 largely due to the Selective Employment Tax. The point is that now at least half of the civilian labour force is employed in services and administration. This, too, is a phenomenon common to all major capitalist countries.

Within this development and of fairly recent origin, are those workers who are technicians, research workers and techno-bureaucrats who work in the advanced technological sectors of the society. There are no separate figures for this group but there is evidence that it is increasing in size, again in all major capitalist countries.

From a cursory examination of the development of the labour force in Britain it is clear that it was continually intruding into new activities, that it always had a new section and that each new section altered the balance of class struggle perspectives of the whole. In this respect there has been no trend in any particular direction nor is it possible to evaluate the impact of changes. Who can say whether the dilution of craft skills had more or less significance for the class struggle than the urbanisation of rural labour or than the growth in administrative and service workers? In this process of perpetual change how is it possible to single out one particular development as Serge Mallet did and state that here is a New Working Class?[5] Mallet looked largely at what might be a one-off event in France in May–June 1968. In Britain the leaders in the class struggle since 1970 have been the miners and engineering workers, not new sections in the labour force.

VI. TRADE UNIONISM AS AN INDEX OF IDENTITY

The sellers of labour power must be seen in the first instance as a totality. They are distributed amongst many and varied occupational activities and they have been recruited from different sources – through the reproduction of the established labour force, from the bourgeoisie in a small way but more importantly from the declining petty-bourgeoisie. Women have increasingly been drawn into the labour force, as have immigrants from the former British Commonwealth countries. Thus the labour force represents a mixture of social backgrounds and aspirations as well as of ethnic groups. The mixture has not been a random one. Women and ethnic minorities have been exploited as sources of cheap labour in areas of industrial activity under-manned by white indigenous males. The bourgeoisie and petty-bourgeoisie have moved, as far as possible, into activities consistent with their social aspirations. The labour markets have been institutionalised to facilitate this distribution. In other words, it has not been an accident of history.

The distribution and redistribution of the labour force has occurred within an ideological setting which has conferred status on work which is not manual. It has glorified brainwork over handwork and the pure over the practical. Knowledge has been reified.[6] There has been a hierarchy of status emphases within the area designated as brainwork. As I stated earlier, the frontiers of the area were not left in the custody of ideology. The notion of superiority was backed by real privileges, again distributed in an hierarchical fashion, which took the form of higher incomes, greater security of employment, shorter working hours, more pleasurable working conditions, better social amenities, more substantial pensions. Being classified as a brainworker even at the margin clearly paid.

Yet despite the varied sources of recruitment to the labour force, the ideological climate of its development, the facilities granted to institutionalise the protection of privileges, the contradictions at the point of production which pose the interests of workers against each other, there is evidence of a growing commonness in the reactions of sellers of labour power to their respective situations. This evidence lies in the spread of trade unionism.

I mean by trade unionism not the act of taking out a membership card of a trade union but the propensity to take collective action against employers to protect and improve their living standards. It is important to distinguish between trade unionism which involves a rejection of the dominant values of the capitalist system and trade unions which as institutions possess the methods and the values of the system. When a group of workers decide to practice trade unionism they do so because their perception of their relationship with their employer has altered. Their action is a rejection of individualism for collectivism, of inequality between themselves and within the confines of their perceived labour markets for equality, of authoritarianism for democracy. It is this whether they recognise it or not.

It is not the case, as many have argued, that consciousness is contained in compartments. That there is 'trade union consciousness' in its own box, useful for immediate needs but useless for altering the system, and that there is 'class consciousness' of a different order, in its own box, labelled 'for revolutionary purposes only'. Consciousness is a complex, contradictory phenomenon. Consider, for example, the case of the dockers I mentioned earlier whose activities are characterised by intensive solidarity, militant action, an awareness of the political implications of their actions, as was shown during the campaign against the Industrial Relations Act in 1971, and a marked racist attitude. There is, moreover, no direct correlation between a consciousness, or awareness of a situation and experience. This raises the question of what is meant by class struggle for collective action can have class consequences without being taken through an awareness of class identity. The miners' strike in 1974 was about a wage increase, regarded by some as a simple case of economism, but the context of the strike transformed its character. When a group of workers go on strike the outcome depends on who else is striking at the same time, the degree and type of government involvement, the intensity of the contradictions in the society as a whole, on the possibility or impossibility of achieving even limited objectives within the system, and on the contradictions dividing the bourgeoisie and its support mechanism. It is not possible to state *a priori* what the political outcome of a civil service strike for a salary increase would be without a knowledge of the context of the strike. In these days of high government involvement in economic affairs as a way of solving constant crises and protecting the system, it may be enough for workers to take collective action for profound political consequences to result. It may be sufficient for many groups to search for their own limited objectives in a system incapable of satisfying any for its structure to be disrupted. Not only is the meaning of class struggle a question, but also class consciousness.

If this analysis has any validity, it means that the spread of trade unionism in general and into hitherto largely unaffected labour markets in particular, has important implications for the class struggle. Moreover it confirms the basic identity of all sellers of labour power with each other. There is possibly no area of industrial activity in Britain where trade unionism is not present. The labour markets which have been the most resistant, namely those influenced by the non-manual ethic, are now the fastest growing areas of trade unionism. Few sections of these markets are uninfluenced by the macro-forces of technology and changes in the level of employment which have had such decisive effects upon the consciousness of manual workers. Indeed the protective measures against trade unionism set up by employers, such as stability of employment, higher relative earnings, more congenial working conditions and the like have either been eroded or equalised. Full employment gave security of employment to virtually all workers. Unemployment on its present (1977) scale hits supervisory, management and administrative staffs as it does workers in other labour markets. The enhanced bargaining power of organised workers during full employment enabled them to share in the fringe benefits hitherto the preserve of those workers described as staff. Technology has removed many physical distinctions between different types of workers. Clerks and administrative workers may now use machines dressed in white coats while steel production workers sit in relatively clean cubicles and press buttons. Mike Cooley has emphasised that technological change and the use of computers in the conventionally described non-manual areas of work have enabled employers to maximise output through rationalising effort. Work is being organized in a systematic way, pace is being regulated, attempts are being made to introduce shift-work, for non-manual workers as it has always been done in the field of production. Indeed Cooley goes so far as to generalise that 'the more technological change and computerisation enters white-collar areas, the more workers in those areas will become proletarianised'.[7]

Cooley shows that changes in the labour process act as a catalyst on attitudes and transform them. In other words, they make the reality of everyday life inconsistent with conventional explanations; they break down the dominance of the dominant ideology. They have the levelling consequences.

CONCLUSION

Where then does this analysis lead? Clearly we must avoid making false analytical distinctions between sellers of labour power. Bourgeois categories are real enough as instruments of social control but they are false in that they neglect the structural determinants of behaviour and can never, therefore, explain changes in behaviour. But, it might be said, are not the middle classes the repositories of political reaction? Is it not there that support for the system as it is mainly stems? This kind of question has an ideological basis. The dominant ideology not only encourages the categorisation of people but gives the categories political attributes. If people are encouraged to believe that they invariably support the system then might they not do so in time of crisis. It is clear from my analysis that nothing is sacred, that the transforming qualities of changes in the labour process can pervert or destroy conventional political attitudes almost overnight. We live in a dynamic system where anything is possible. Moreover, even visible evidence does not support the conventional view of the political position of 'middle classes.' They are not the sole repositories of political reaction. The contradictions which beset all labour markets are reflected in contrasting political attitudes. The problem of political reaction is a general one. After all, it is estimated that approximately 30 per cent of conventionally defined manual workers vote Conservative. As some groups, like miners and dockers, are predominantly anti-Conservative it must mean that some are as predominantly for them as the middle-classes are supposed to be.

There is other evidence of the differential dispersion of political attitudes amongst labour markets. There have been increasing illustrations of management identification with other workers in plants threatened with closure. The local branch of the Steel Industry Management Association (SIMA) at the Shotton, North Wales iron and steel plant is an integral part of the Shotton Action Committee formed to prevent the closure of the plant by a work-in if necessary. SIMA has a record of close identification with employers. Yet on this occasion the SIMA representative on the Action Committee was chairman of the sub-committee entrusted with the task of working out the details of a work-in. This could, of course, be described as a class 'position' within a particular historically determined context. But this would refute the possibility of transformation which we, as Marxists, must always anticipate. All groups, in fact, adopt positions in the class struggle which are contradictory over time. It is only necessary to follow the miners ballot on wages issues from 1971 to the present for illustrations of sharp inconsistencies.

But are there no class distinctions worth making within the class of sellers of labour power? What about the categories of productive and non-productive labour? Firstly, as I intimated earlier, a distinction has to be real in terms of its influence on behaviour to be worth making in this context. It is difficult enough to make consistent analytical categories between productive and non-productive as Nicos Poulantzas's attempts have shown. There is no agreement amongst Marxists as to who should fall in which category. The empirical task of categorisation is greater. But even if it were possible, do the labour process experiences vary sufficiently between the two categories to give rise to different perceptions of reality and different modes of behaviour? This has not been proved. On the contrary empirical evidence is against it. The same applies to the other categorisations such as that made by Poulantzas between 'mental' and 'manual' labour. Poulantzas argues that 'mental' labour has access to the 'secret knowledge' of the production process and into this category he almost, but not quite, places the conventional white-collar workers. He defies, however, the reality of power in the production process and is relying on formal bureaucratic divisions. No one who knows about the involvement of skilled production workers in the steel industry and if the extent to which they are decision-makers could generate corresponding illusions about 'mental' and 'manual' divisions.

We are therefore left with a single class of employees divided into largely ideologically determined labour markets within each of which is a uniform labour process. These markets have their contradictions which are transforming them and altering their relations with each other. The criterion for identifying the markets are source of recruitment, the imposition of qualifications, the stipulations about training and devices for achieving and maintaining insularity. Such labour in markets can easily be distinguished for agricultural workers, for dockers, for miners, for administrative class civil servants, for doctors, lawyers, dentists and the like in combination. These markets have no social ranking and no hierarchy. They have no names behind which we can slot people. Their acceptance involves the rejection of a multiple class structure but it enables us to see in detail how the process of class formation proceeds.

REFERENCES

1. See 'Language of "Class" in Early Nineteenth century England' by Asa Briggs in *Essays in Labour History*, Asa Briggs and John Saville (eds), 1960.

2. Goldthorpe, J. H., Lockwood, D. *et al.*, *The Affluent Worker* (3 vols), Cambridge University Press, 1968–9.
3. *Classes in Contemporary Capitalism*, London, 1976, p. 14.
4. Ibid., pp. 15–16.
5. In *The New Working Class*, London, 1975.
6. See 'Ideology of/in Contemporary Physics' by Jean Marc Livy-Leblond, in *The Radicalisation of Science*, Hilary and Steven Rose (eds), London, 1976.
7. 'Contradictions of Science and Technology' by Mike Cooley, in *The Political Economy of Science*, Hilary and Steven Rose (eds), London, 1976, p. 78.

THEORY AND POLITICS IN THE IDENTIFICATION OF THE WORKING CLASS

Alan Hunt

In this paper I want to tackle three related tasks. First, I will attempt to identify the political implications of the current debate which revolves around the identification of social classes. Second, I will present a critique of Nicos Poulantzas's approach to the identification of the working class. Third, I want to suggest an alternative approach which can, I hope, make a contribution to both the political and theoretical problems generated by the discussion of the Marxist theory of class.

I. THE POLITICS OF CLASS IDENTIFICATION

It is not without significance that a discussion is now taking place within the socialist movement about the identification of social classes, and more specifically, about the identification of the working class. It is important to consider why this debate is taking place, and what its political significance is.

Within the history of the revolutionary movement the question of 'what is the working class?' has not until relatively recently (the turning point is perhaps to be found in the 1930s) been a pressing problem. From Marx through to Lenin the concept of the 'working class' was relatively non-problematic. The working class was identified as the industrial or factory proletariat. Throughout the 'classical' period of Marxist theory the problem which presented itself was the relationship between the working class and other social classes. Specifically within the Leninist tradition the central political problematic was the relationship between the working class and the peasantry.[1]

The problem of the identification of the boundaries of the working class came to the forefront in the period after 1917 when the prospects of the Russian Revolution were presented as depending upon the fate of the revolutionary movement in the heartlands of industrial capitalism in Western Europe. Here the central contradiction presented itself in terms of the massive size of a proletariat which had, however, proved unable to produce the rapid repercussions to the Russian October that were so widely anticipated. The problem was not presented in any developed form until the triumph of German fascism forced the Communist movement to focus attention on the relations *within* the working class. The transition was from the 'third period', with its exclusively ideological treatment of the working class, expressed in the characterisation of social democracy as 'social fascism', to the period of the 'united front' and 'popular front'.

Since the 1930s the general strategies of the Communist movement in Western Europe have revolved around the problem of *class alliances*. They have centred on the fundamentally Gramscian project of the realisation of the hegemonic influence of the working class, which encompasses both the realisation of that class itself and the extension of its influence and leadership over other social classes. For most of the period this perspective has coexisted with an alternative political perspective, one which in its fundamentals constitutes an insurrectionary strategy. The central, indeed almost exclusive, emphasis is upon the industrial or factory proletariat. This is seen as the 'fundamentally revolutionary class' which in leading the final assault upon the capitalist order will be able to take with it the rest of the working population. It is important to stress that these two perspectives are not necessarily incompatible. The greater the emphasis on the leading role of the industrial working class, the greater is the tendency to regard all other classes or strata as, at best, temporary or unstable allies, and the more does the associated political strategy take on an insurrectionary character.

Despite the central role of class and classes in Marxist theory and political strategy, there are important respects in which it has remained underdeveloped and unexplored. It is important to bear in mind that the revolutionary application of Marxist theory, particularly in the two great revolutionary experiences of Russia and China, both required and indeed produced very specific and profound analyses of class structure and class relations. Lenin's *The Development of Capitalism in Russia*[2] and Mao Tse-tung's *Analysis of the Classes in Chinese Society* and his *Report on an Investigation of the Peasant Movement in Hunan*[3] played an important role in the framing of the long-term strategies of the Bolshevik Party and the Chinese Communist Party.

In Western Europe, particularly in Britain, the nature of the working class has largely been taken for granted; it has been seen as synonymous with factory workers. Additionally Marxists were for a long period on the defensive against attacks on the very concept of class. Their response was to insist, in general terms, upon the relevance and validity of the class concept, against a range of positions which directly or indirectly undermined the Marxist theory of class. As a consequence of this embattled position there was little space or scope for the consideration of issues or problems *within* the Marxist theory of class.

The absence of such theoretical discussions has had its impact in both theory and political practice. For example, the British Left has made use of an underdeveloped, and often contradictory, analysis of class structure. The term 'working class' is often used in an indiscriminate way to refer either to factory workers or to all wage-earners, and it is rarely specified which usage is being employed. Not infrequently use has been made of a three class model which goes a long way towards accepting the concept of a 'middle class'.[4] A final example is the formulation of the concept 'anti-monopoly alliance' as presented in the current version of the *British Road to Socialism*,[5] which defines the alliance as: 'embracing all working people. Thus workers in factories, offices, professions, working farmers, producers and consumers, owner-occupiers and tenants, housewives, young people and students, pensioners, workers in the peace movement, and those active in defence of democracy.' This definition does not distinguish between class categories, occupations, and social and political movements.

In the current period there have been important signs of a developing concern to carry forward the analysis of class and class structure within the framework of Marxist theory. In doing this it is of paramount importance that the political implications are kept to the forefront. These can be presented somewhat schematically as a choice between a 'broad' and a 'narrow' definition of the working class.

The 'broad' definition conventionally takes the working class as being composed of all those who sell their labour-power, and thus embraces all wage and salary earners. Presented in this way the working class, in Britain and most other developed capitalist societies, constitutes the overwhelming majority of the population. The strategic questions which flow from a 'broad' definition focus attention on the question of the *unity of the working class*. The preponderant numerical weight of the working class, if politically and ideologically united, makes possible a non-insurrectionary strategy of socialist revolution. The central questions become those of identifying the different sections or fractions of the working class, in order to come to an understanding of the conditions for the realisation of the unity of the class.

However such a 'broad' definition is not without major problems. To utilise the single criteria of wages embraces sections of the population which every political instinct makes us reject as members of the working class; senior management, military personnel, and leading state functionaries are obvious examples. I discuss later the criteria by which such sections can be differentiated.

The 'narrow' definition, specified as productive labourers or as factory workers, presents a totally different political perspective. Defined in this way the working class constitutes not only a small, but also a declining proportion of the total population in advanced capitalist societies.[6] Under these circumstances the prospect of socialist revolution becomes dependent upon the creation of class alliances with *other* social classes, who by definition have class interests different from those of the working class. Such alliances are of course important, and indeed Poulantzas explicitly discusses the prospects for an alliance with the 'new petty bourgeoisie', but they are necessarily limited, and, to a greater or lesser extent, unstable. The politics that result from such a perspective will exhibit a tendency to emphasise an insurrectionary strategy. Similarly the 'narrow' and the 'broad' definitions will result in very different interpretations of the traditional Leninist theses concerning the 'leading role of the proletariat' and the role of 'the Party'.

One conclusion is inescapable. The identification of the working class cannot be regarded as an exclusively theoretical exercise. It is a profoundly political question that goes to the very heart of the formation of revolutionary strategy.

II. POULANTZAS AND THE IDENTIFICATION OF THE WORKING CLASS

Nicos Poulantzas has provided the most rigorous presentation of the 'narrow' definition of the working class, as composed of manual productive labourers, and which expressly excludes large sections of wage-earners who are identified as constituting the 'new petty bourgeoisie'.[7] I want to concentrate upon a number of aspects of his treatment, without embarking upon an exhaustive discussion of his work;[8] in particular I want to concentrate upon the structure of his argument.

Poulantzas's starting-point is to insist that classes cannot be defined exclusively at the economic level, and he stresses the importance of the ideological and political level in determining social classes. He devotes the greatest attention to the economic level, and later I shall argue that, despite his insistence on the importance of politics and ideology, he produces an essentially economistic treatment of social classes. It is therefore appropriate to start by examining his views concerning the economic identification of the working class.

Derivation of Classes from Production Relations

Production relations provide the starting point for the Marxist analysis of social classes. 'In the social production of their life, men enter into definite relations that are indispensable and independent of their will, relations of production that correspond to a definite stage of development of their material productive forces.'[9] As Poulantzas expresses it, the distribution into social classes is determined by the relations of production. So far no problems arise, but it is necessary to follow Poulantzas's line of argument in order to bring out the content of the relationship between social classes and production relations.

Production relations have a dual character; there is first a relation between persons and nature (the labour process), and relations between people (the social relations of production). It is this latter which he describes as 'relations between men and other men, class relations.'[10] Next he examines the first aspect of this double relationship, and, in particular, focuses upon the relation between producers and the productive forces. It is this relationship which he insists 'defines the exploited class in the relations of production'.[11] From this he arrives at his general definition of the working class, namely:

the working class in the capitalist mode of production is that which performs the productive labour of that mode of production.[12]

This method of arriving at the definition of the working class produces an economistic or technicist definition of the working class. Poulantzas correctly insists that production relations are constituted from the unity of what may be expressed as men-nature relationships with men-men relationships, and that within this duality it is the men-men relationships (the relations of production) which are dominant over the men—nature relationships (labour process). It should be stressed that, as we have seen, he has suggested that the men—men relationships are synonymous with *class relations*. Yet his identification of the central determinant of the working class is to be *derived from relations within the labour process*. The consequences of this line of argument should be noted. It does violence to one of the most important general features of Marx's treatment of class, which insists on the essentially *relational* character of classes; classes do not exist in their own right, but only by virtue of the existence of other classes.[13]

This relational character of the very concept of class stands out very clearly in the famous passage from the *Manifesto of the Communist Party* in which the historical characteristic of class formation is insisted upon.

The proletariat goes through various stages of development. With its birth begins its struggle with the bourgeoisie. At first the contest is carried on by individual labourers, then by the workpeople of a factory . . . At this stage the labourers still form an incoherent mass . . .
But with the development of industry the proletariat not only increases in numbers; it becomes concentrated in greater masses, its strength grows, and it feels that strength more . . . the collisions between individual workmen and individual bourgeois takes more and more the character of collisions between two classes.[14]

The error which Poulantzas commits is to derive his definition from a different conceptual level (namely the productive process) from the one which he himself specifies as dominant (namely, social relations of production). His fallacy is to assert the primacy of the 'social relations of production' but to derive his definition of the working class *exclusively* from the 'labour process'. The result is an economistic or technicist definition of the working class. Rather it should be insisted that relations within the labour process specify the particular role within the prevailing class relations that various forms of labour perform, but they are not the determinants of those class relations.

The result of locating the definition of the working class by reference to the labour process is to diminish the significance attached by Poulantzas to property relations. Property relations within Marx's conceptual framework provide a direct manifestation of the social relations of production.[15] Thus while Poulantzas stresses, quite correctly in my view, the distinction between 'economic ownership' and 'legal ownership', he makes almost no use at all of property relations in his identification of social classes. This is further evidence of the direction that is imposed upon his analysis by his prior decision to accentuate the relations within the labour process.

Productive Labour and Class Relations

The boundary between the working class and the 'new petty bourgeoisie', at the economic level, is provided by the distinction between productive and unproductive labour.[16] It is counterposed to the identification of the working class as those engaging in wage-labour.

It is not wages that define the working class economically . . . Although every worker is a wage-earner, every wage-earner is certainly not a worker, for not every wage-earner is engaged in productive labour.[17]

Let me consider his rejection of the wage-labour criterion before going on to discuss productive labour.

His rejection of the view that the working class may be defined economically in terms of wage relationship, which he labels a social democratic position, rests on the insistence that 'wages are a form of the distribution of the social product',[18] and 'are a juridical form on which the product is divided up according to the contract governing the buying and selling of labour-power'.[19] This equation of wages and 'mode of distribution' predetermines the future course of the argument. After all we know that Marx insisted on the primacy of production over distribution, exchange and consumption.[20] Since Poulantzas has selected his causal determinant (i.e. production of surplus value) from the sphere of production, then it seems to follow that this is preferable to a criteria (i.e. wages) selected from the sphere of distribution. But the whole argument hinges on his assertion that wages are a mode of distribution.

Wages are no more exclusively part of distribution than capital is exclusively related to the sphere of production. Wages are ultimately consumed in the means of reproduction of labour power, but at the outset they are the form in which capital, specifically variable capital, is expended in the purchase of wage labour. Simply to label wages as a form of distribution thus obscures the fact that wages like capital undertake a cyclical progression. But Marx observes that the wage relation 'never itself assumes the form of revenue, revenue of the labourer, until it has first confronted this labourer in the form of capital'.[21] At this stage, therefore, I simply want to suggest that Poulantzas has not succeeded in dispensing with the criterion of wage-labour as a determinant of class boundary as simply as he thinks.

Let us now turn to his usage of the productive/unproductive labour distinction. I do not wish to enter into too many of the intricacies of the debate about productive labour.[22] I want to focus attention on what seems to be the central question: is it correct to use Marx's distinction between productive and unproductive labour to define the economic identification of the working class?

A few words need to be said about the implications of this question. If its use as determinant of the definition of the working class at the economic level is correct, then important sections of wage-earners are *by definition* excluded from membership of the working class; in particular it would exclude all workers in the commercial sector,[23] and all state employees, other than those engaged in 'productive' nationalised industries. It is important to recognise that Marx's theses concerning productive and unproductive labour are not as unproblematic as Poulantzas's treatment suggests;[24] this can be seen if we hesitate for a moment before casting state employees into the category of unproductive workers. State employees are paid out of revenue and, following Marx, this renders them unproductive. However, looked at from the criteria of its relation to the production of surplus-value the result is not so self-evident. State revenue expenditure on – for example, health and education – is an increasingly important component of real wages, and as such the labour expended can be regarded as contributing to the reproduction of variable capital. This does not 'prove' that state employees are 'productive', but it does suggest that the application of the productive/unproductive distinction is more problematic than Poulantzas indicates.

It should also be noted that Poulantzas's usages of the

productive/unproductive distinction is itself not strictly faithful to Marx's own. Poulantzas's definition is as follows: 'productive labour, in the capitalist mode of production, is labour that produces surplus-value *while directly reproducing the material elements that serve as the substratum of the relation of exploitation*'.[25]

But Marx himself quite strenuously rejected the criteria of material production, and indeed devoted considerable attention to attacking Adam Smith for including this within his definition of productive labour.[26]

This 'narrowness' in the working definition of productive labour particularly manifests itself when Poulantzas discusses service workers. He contents himself with categorising them as unproductive because their labour is exchanged for revenue. His error lies in viewing the relationship from the standpoint of the consumer/purchaser of services. From the standpoint of the capitalist, who invests both labour-power and capital in the production of the service, the workers in the service industry are paid from variable capital (and not from revenue), and the service produced is sold as a commodity (irrespective of whether it has a material form or not) and, as a consequence, surplus-value is produced which is appropriated by the capitalist. A simple illustration serves to make the point; if I am in the habit of having my windows cleaned, it makes no difference to me (as consumer) if I engage a self-employed window-cleaner or use a window-cleaning firm; in either case I expend my income, and the service is paid for out of 'revenue'. But it does not follow that the position of the individual who carries out the window-cleaning is the same. The employee of the window-cleaning firm is paid out of variable capital advanced by the capitalist owner, and his labour yields surplus-value which is appropriated. The result must be that we should regard the employed window-cleaner as a productive labourer.[27]

What Poulantzas does not recognise about Marx's discussion of services is its historical dimension. It was the field of material production that the capitalist mode of production first conquered, whereas it only advanced more slowly into the field of service production; indeed that process is still not fully completed. While Poulantzas claims to root his discussion in the monopoly stage of the capitalist mode of production, his formalistic application of the productive/unproductive labour distinction results in him being unable to analyse important changes in the social relations of production.

The same criticism applies to Poulantzas's treatment of Marx's concept of the 'collective labourer', and its result in his conclusion that technicians, engineers and scientists are not members of the working class. It is important to note some of the particular characteristics of his argument. His treatment of the 'collective labourer' is conflated with his discussion of the division between mental and manual labour, which he sees as being the central feature of the ideological relations within the social division of labour. This presentation has the effect of diverting attention from the significance of the 'collective labourer' at the economic level; this is all the more surprising because he himself admits that 'the division between manual and mental labour in no way coincides with the division between productive and unproductive labour'.[28] Having up to this stage in his argument operated, as has been shown, with a very narrow and technical treatment of productive labour, he accuses anyone who attaches significance to the collective labourer of economic reductionism.

Let me briefly indicate the importance of the concept of the collective labourer in the identification of social classes. With the historical development of the capitalist mode of production:

The product ceases to be the direct product of the individual, and becomes a social product, produced in common by a collective labourer, i.e. by a combination of workmen, each of whom takes only a part, greater or less, in the manipulation of the subject of their labour. As the co-operative character of the labour-process becomes more and more marked, so, as a necessary consequence, does our notion of productive labour, and of its agent the productive labourer, become extended. In order to labour productively, it is no longer necessary for you to do manual work yourself; enough, if you are an organ of the collective labourer, and perform one of its subordinate functions.[29]

It is important to insist that collective labour becomes increasingly important, and that it is an essential concept for understanding the modern capitalist production process. The development of mechanisation, automation and computerisation at the technical level, each marks a further development of collective labour.

The concept of the collective labourer has a direct impact on the distinction between productive and unproductive labour. In the first place many wage-earners whose role in the labour process at an early stage of capitalist development have been unproductive must now be regarded as part of the collective labourer. Additionally the material conditions of the labour activities of unproductive workers comes to be transformed through the changes in the productive techniques such that, as Braverman argues, they 'share in the subjugation and oppression that characterises the lives of the productive workers'.[30]

Marx in his discussion of the impact of machines and mechanisation notes their profound impact on the labour process.

Labour no longer appears so much to be included within the production process; rather, the human being comes to relate more as watchman and regulator to the production process itself . . . He steps to the side of the production process instead of being its chief actor . . . It is, in a word, the development of the social individual which appears as the great foundation-stone of production and of wealth.[31]

Without exploring the issues raised in any detail, it is clear that there are profound implications for the concept of productive labour on which Poulantzas seeks to rest his identification of the working class. This certainly casts very considerable doubt on his treatment of the role of scientists and technicians in the labour process. His conclusion that they are members of the 'new petty bourgeoisie' is arrived at by making a switch from an analysis at the economic level to the ideological level, in which he posits the distinction between mental and manual labour as residing within the ideological level. It is clear from Marx's treatment that he regarded mental labour as a part, and indeed an increasingly important part, of the labour process itself. Poulantzas asserts that scientists and technicians simply reproduce the dominant ideology within the productive process, and that 'their mental labour, separated from manual labour, represents the exercise of political relations in the despotism of the factory'.[32] This comes nowhere near grasping their significance within the modern productive process.

It is necessary to stress that if we were to accept the productive/unproductive labour distinction for identifying the working class economically, then it would throw up a host of anomalies. For example, a teacher in a private school is a productive worker 'when in addition to belabouring the heads of his scholars, he works like a horse to enrich the school proprietor',[33] while a teacher in a state school is not a productive worker. Again, a shop assistant stacking tins on the shelves of a supermarket is a productive worker whereas a colleague who operates the till is not. Drivers of goods trains are certainly productive labourers, but it is less certain that their work-mates manning passenger trains are. These anomalies do not in themselves disprove Poulantzas's thesis but they do point us towards the source of his error.

There is no dispute that the discovery and analysis of surplus value plays a central part in Marxist economic theory. What, however, is contentious is the insistence that this concept plays a determining role in the economic definition of the working class. The concept of surplus-value, and hence the distinction between productive and unproductive labour which is drawn from it, plays a fundamental role in the object of inquiry towards which Marx's economic writings are directed. That object is provided in Marx's sub-title to 'Capital', namely 'the critique of political economy'. The central importance of the concept of surplus-value in that context does not imply or require that this concept is central when directed towards a different object of inquiry, namely that of class analysis.[34] Indeed when Marx in the famous 'unfinished' chapter at the end of *Capital* III turns to classes as the object of inquiry he starts out on a line of arguments quite untenable from Poulantzas's position, in that he advances a three class model (capitalists, landowners and workers) distinguished by their sources of income. It is not therefore self-evident that the concept 'surplus-value' yields the means of distinguishing between social classes within the capitalist mode of production.

Any fundamental criteria of class determination must meet one essential test. Does it succeed in revealing the most fundamental and pervasive boundaries within the social structure? It must reveal real differences between the classes and their members. Does the productive/unproductive labour criteria reveal such real cleavages? As we have already argued, the use of this criteria fails to distinguish meaningly between positions in the labour process. The application of the productive/unproductive distinction imposes a divide between positions which share many common and important characteristics. Productive and unproductive labourers share the following important characteristics: they are both exploited through the extraction of surplus labour; they both have antagonistic relationships with their employers; the value of their labour power is determined in the same way, that is by the cost of its reproduction; their labour power is purchased by their respective employers for the same purpose, namely the realisation of profit. Given these fundamental similarities between productive and unproductive labourers the fact that they can be distinguished by reference to the production of surplus-value does not provide sufficient grounds to put them into different, and therefore, opposed, classes. Further, and it is a point that I will not develop but it is nevertheless important, even less is there reason to place unproductive workers into a class designated as the 'new petty bourgeoisie', whose only connection with Marx's category, the 'petty bourgeoisie', is to be found at the political and ideological levels, and even here I want to argue later that the marriage that Poulantzas arranges between the 'new' and the 'traditional petty bourgeoisie' is very much a shotgun affair.

This argument that the concept of productive labour does not in itself provide us with criteria for locating a class boundary between productive and unproductive workers also provides the basic context for Erik Olin Wright's objection to Poulantzas. Wright asks: does the surplus-value criteria reveal fundamentally *different class interests*, at the economic level between productive and unproductive workers? I believe that Wright asks the correct question, but that his answer that both productive and unproductive labourers have a common economic interest in socialism is less than satisfactory.[35] The concept of 'class interests' raise a number of serious problems which I do not wish to introduce.[36] The immediate point to be made against Wright is that to argue that the working class has an interest in socialism cannot simply be a statement about economic interests but necessarily involves the political level as well.

The most substantial argument that points to the possibility of conflicting economic interests between productive and unproductive workers is that unproductive workers can be said to 'live off' the surplus value created by productive workers. There is undoubtedly textual authority in Marx for such a position.[37] There is present within Marx an alternative strand of analysis which emphasises that the labour of the unproductive worker is exploited and that 'while it does not create surplus-value, enables him (the capitalist) to appropriate surplus-value . . . It is, therefore, a source of profit for him.'[38] This is not the occasion to explore the question fully, but to make one comment: the labour of unproductive workers is as *necessary* as that of productive labourers to the reproduction and expansion of capital. We need to avoid the essentially moralistic argument of identifying productive labour with 'useful labour'. The productive/unproductive labour distinction is not synonymous with a distinction between useful and useless labour. As Marx observes:

The designation of labour as *productive labour* has absolutely nothing to do with the *determinant content* of that labour, its special utility, or the particular use-value in which it manifests itself. The *same* kind of labour may be *productive* or *unproductive*.[39]

It is now possible to state a general conclusion concerning the application of the distinction between productive and unproductive labour in the identification of classes at the economic level. The analysis developed by Poulantzas does not reveal any grounds upon which we should accord the distinction any primacy in the location of a class boundary. While it is important in drawing distinctions between the location of various types of labour, it does not disclose a class boundary between the working class, and some other and opposed class.

The Political and Ideological Determination of Classes

We have already noted that Poulantzas insists that classes cannot be identified exclusively at the economic level. It is necessary to examine the way in which he treats the role of the political and ideological levels in the structural determination of classes. I want to take issue, not with the insistence that classes cannot be identified exclusively at the economic level, but rather with his treatment of the role of the political and the ideological in the determination of social classes.

The discussion of the role of the ideological and political levels is not simply a problem in the determination of classes; it raises a set of problems which have provided the central problematic of contemporary discussions within Marxist theory. The central concern of what has become labelled 'Western Marxism'[40] has been a reaction against the economic determinism of the Marxism of both the Second International[41] and the Third International. This reaction has taken its starting points from those passages of Marx and particularly of Engels[42] which point to the 'relative autonomy' of politics and ideology. This has been the central organising element in the Althusserian project, and the debates which that has engendered, and within which Poulantzas's own work has been an important contribution. And the most general level this substance of the discussion is provided by the problems posed in terms of the relationship between 'base' and 'superstructure'.

This fundamental question cannot be resolved in isolation from its wider context. But Poulantzas's attempt to tackle the problem in the context of class analysis serves to identify some of its problems.

Poulantzas's treatment of the ideological and political levels in the determination of social classes is within the tradition that is anxious to assert their 'relative autonomy'. Yet his treatment, despite his extensive discussion of the non-economic levels, does not realise this objective. His analysis is, in the final analysis, profoundly economistic. The boundary of the working class is specified or determined at the economic level (the productive labour criteria), and this economically prescribed boundary is simply *reinforced* at the political and ideological level. In his treatment of the ideological and politically determination of social class he continues to operate exclusively with his single economic criteria. In other words, while purporting to insist on the 'relative autonomy' of the political and ideological, in practice they serve simply to underline or reinforce the determination at the economic level. The end result is an economistic analysis buttressed at the political and ideological levels.[43] The consequence is that Poulantzas, despite his claims to the contrary, is not able to establish the specific effectivity of the political and the ideological.

The context in which I want to discuss Poulantzas's treatment of the ideological and political levels is with respect to his treatment of the 'new petty bourgeoisie'. It is fair to accuse him of fitting his argument to meet his predetermined conclusion concerning the economic identification of the working class. His insistence that non-productive labourers are not members of the working class presents him with a 'problem'. If non-productive labourers are not members of the working class, what class are they members of? Poulantzas has already excluded the possibility that they are 'outside' the class structure since he has already rejected the thesis developed by the French Communist Party that they are an 'intermediate strata'. Hence he is forced by the logic of his own analysis either to identify them as an entirely 'new' class (but to do so would imply that the transformation of modern capitalism constituted a new mode of production) or, alternatively, to align them with an existing class. It is this latter solution that he pursues. The 'petty bourgeoisie' is the only available alternative class, but to align non-productive labourers with the petty bourgeoisie is not self-evident. As he himself recognises 'these two large groups occupy different and utterly dissimilar positions in production'.[44] His resolution of this apparent contradiction is to insist that, despite the different economic positions, the 'new' and the 'traditional' petty bourgeoisie have 'the same effects at the political and ideological level'.[45]

The proof that is offered to support the contention that the new and the traditional petty bourgeoisie can be linked is that they have 'the same political and ideological characteristics'. This connection is established by attributing certain ideological and political characteristics to the 'new petty bourgeoisie'. This process is nothing more than a schematic labelling, which attributes a range of attitudes to the 'new petty bourgeoisie', which are presented as manifesting individualism, attachment to the *status quo*, fear of revolution, adherence to the myth of personal advancement, acceptance of bourgeois aspirations, etc. Upon this basis he arrives at the conclusion that 'these *common* ideological-political characteristics provide sufficient grounds for considering that these two ensembles with different places in the economy constitute a relatively unified class, the petty bourgeoisie'.[46]

This is a totally unsatisfactory argument. It makes use of a procedure quite alien to the Marxist method, namely that of ascription which imposes an apparent uniformity of ideological and political position. The empirical reality of the non-productive workers offers a much richer and more diverse set of ideological and political positions which requires a more searching analysis than the method of arbitrary ascription allows. Poulantzas provides nothing more than a caricature which is a commonplace in bourgeois subjectivist analysis.

Poulantzas marshals a number of supporting theoretical arguments to sustain this analysis. There are two major strands which inject a primary criteria for both the political and ideological levels. At the ideological level he makes use of the distinction between mental and manual labour, and at the political level between relations of domination and subordination, specifically concerning the role of supervision and management. I shall want to say something in my conclusion about how these levels relate to the economic identification of classes, and therefore without in any way repudiating their importance, I want to comment briefly on the way in which Poulantzas makes use of them.

First, with respect to the division between mental and manual labour. Poulantzas places considerable emphasis upon Marx's observation that the social division of labour between mental and manual labour takes on an antagonistic character in the capitalist labour process.[47] From this he argues that it gives rise to an ideological relation of privilege and of domination through the monopoly of knowledge over manual labourers. He cites in evidence Gramsci's characterisation of engineers and technicians as 'modern intellectuals'.[48] Such an analysis, in particular the way in which Gramsci is used, is ahistorical, in that it takes no account of the changes in the labour process under monopoly capitalism.

The division between mental and manual labour can perhaps be better understood as having ideological *effects* which are not simply the result of the technical division of labour, and are therefore not necessary or inevitable consequences of the division between mental and manual labour itself. If mental labourers form part of the 'collective labourer' as I have argued, then we can go on to say that their ideological characteristics may remain problematic or contradictory; but it is important to insist that this is a *possible* and not a necessary consequence of the division of labour. In other words Poulantzas has a determinist conception of ideology as being determined by the technical or economic level.[49]

The division between mental and manual labour plays a key role for Poulantzas also with respect to the political level. The political relations within the production process take the form of the dominance of the working class by those carrying out the work of management or supervision. He attaches little importance to the distinction that Marx makes between those elements of management and supervision that are necessary to a given technical level of production, i.e. tasks of organisation and co-ordination, and those that are particular to its form within the capitalist mode of production. He presents supervision as embodying the dominance of capitalist political relations over the productive process. Managers and supervisors 'occupy the actual place of capital'.[50] But, as Wright correctly observes: 'It is one thing to say that supervision has a political dimension and another to say that supervision is itself political relations within production.'[51]

The consequences of this error are made more serious when we note Poulantzas's failure to recognise the extent of the penetration of supervisory relations into the labour process. Large sections of manual labourers carry out some element of supervision over the labour of others. What is absent in Poulantzas's treatment is any criteria for distinguishing between the form and extent of supervisory activity which, at both the economic and political levels, separates such wage-labourers from the working class.

III. TOWARDS A SOLUTION

I want now to put forward an attempted solution to the problem of class identification, and to conclude by drawing the political implications that flow from this presentation.

The Marxist concept of class bears a direct relationship to his central concept of 'social relations of production'.

It is not with 'production' that political economy deals, but with the social relations of men in production. Once these social relations have been ascertained and thoroughly analysed, the place in production of every class, and, consequently, the share they get of the national consumption, are *thereby* defined.[52]

Classes may, therefore, be defined as social aggregates that occupy common positions within the social relations of production.

We are therefore presented with the necessity of examining Marx's concept 'social relations of production'. This concept nowhere received systematic elaboration by Marx himself. Indeed it is interesting to note that this concept has received very little scrutiny in more recent Marxist discussions. Even some of the recent rigorous excursions into the theoretical framework of Marxism, such as those by Althusser, Balibar[53] and, in Britain, by Hindess and Hirst,[54] have not devoted any sustained attention to this concept. A useful starting point is provided by Poulantzas himself[55] where he points out that Marx used two similar, but different, concepts interchangeably, namely, *relations of production* (which also appears as 'production relations'), and *social relations of production*. As often happens with Marxist concepts we come to 'learn' them, that is through practice we come to be able to use them in the appropriate contexts without stopping to consider what they 'mean' or designate.

I agree with Poulantzas, and the same point is made by Carchedi,[56] that it is important to distinguish between these concepts. Since this distinction is not provided by Marx himself we must proceed with some caution. Poulantzas and Carchedi make the following distinction: *production relations* refer to relations between the agents of production and the means of production (i.e. people-nature relations); *social relations of production* refer to relations between agents of production. It is interesting to note that Poulantzas makes almost no use of this distinction in *Classes in Contemporary Capitalism*.

I want to suggest that this distinction is too far-reaching. It has the effect of transforming Marx's interchangeable concepts into ones which have an essentially different subject matter, namely 'relations' (people–things connections) and 'relationships' (connections between people). I will argue that these two concepts of Marx should suggest to us that we need to distinguish between *different levels* within the 'social relations of production'.

It is possible to distinguish between three different levels of the social relations of production; and for the sake of identification I will give these different levels labels, which are however provisional and serve an essentially descriptive function.

We may distinguish between the following three levels:

(*a*) immediate or technical relations of production (corresponding to Marx's concept 'production relations');
(*b*) class relations of production (corresponding to Marx's concept of 'social relations of production'); and
(*c*) general or historical relations of production.

This third level is somewhat tentative, and I merely want to give examples. I think there are three examples that are suggested in Marx's writings; they are, as follows, the sexual division of labour, the division between town and country, and the division between mental and manual labour. This third level, if I am correct in identifying it as such, has the characteristic of extending beyond the limits of any particular mode of production. Thus, for example, the sexual division of labour, while taking a particular form within the capitalist mode of production, predates it in the sense that the social relations which characterise the capitalist mode of production develop within the context of a previously existing sexual division of labour.

I have made it clear that the distinction between the three levels which I have indicated are not expressly present in Marx's writings. But there is present within Marx's texts a quite explicit conception of different levels of the *division of labour*. I want to make one brief comment on the connection between the 'division of labour' and 'social relations of production'. The 'division of labour' was a concept which Marx took over directly from classical political economy, and in developing the concept of 'social relations of production' he started the process of transforming it into a concept appropriate for Marxist theory. Marx made use of distinctions between levels within the division of labour, specifically he distinguished between the 'technical', 'social' and 'general' division of labour. I want, therefore, to suggest that, while it is not possible directly and mechanically to transpose from the terms of the 'division of labour' to 'social relations of production', it is quite proper to suggest that the social relations of production may be divided into different levels.

I want now to return to discuss in more detail the levels of the social relations of production that I have indicated, and in particular to concentrate on the *technical* relations of production and *class* relations of production. It is the distinction between these levels which I wish to argue is central to the analysis of the concept of class.

Technical or immediate relations of production (which correspond to Marx's own concept of 'production relations') are relationships between agents of production that are a direct consequence of the existing productive forces.[57] The given forms of production technique impose upon the agents of production certain forms of co-operation and interaction. Thus, for example, assembly-line production requires certain forms of co-operation between workers in particular numerical combinations and the co-ordination of the rate at which labour activity is performed.

The technical relations are, however, not simply sets of relations between producers, but also, and indeed decisively, include relations between labour and capital, or to be more precise between labourers and those performing the function of capital. The importance of these relations needs to be emphasised. A given productive technique is not in itself the determinant of the relations of production. It is the form that is given to these relations within a particular mode of production that is decisive. It is the determination of the technical relations of production by the class relations which establishes, firstly, the fallacy of attributing a technological determinism to Marxism, and, secondly the dominance of the 'social relations of production'. Marxist analysis does not, and cannot, take as its starting point the productive forces, even the immediate relations of the labour process.

These considerations make it more important to examine what I have called *class relations of production*, which corresponds to Marx's concept of 'social relations of production'. Marx was insistent that the existence of wage labour itself does not constitute the existence of a capitalist mode or production, nor of course does the existence of commodity exchange. Rather it is the generalised existence of the labour-capital relation that is the pre-requisite of a capitalist mode of production.

The process . . . that clears the way for the capitalist system, can be none other than the process that transforms, on the one hand, the social means of subsistence and of production into capital, on the other the immediate producers into wage-labourers.[58]

These processes are not simply the result of the quantitative expansion of commodity exchange within the feudal mode of production. Thus, for example, the emergence of 'free labour' is the result of a definite historical process which involves not only the removal of legal restrictions upon mobility, but the use of state coercion to compel the expropriated peasantry into the labour market.[59]

The significance of these processes is that they give rise to sets of social relations that are generalised throughout society. Irrespective of the locations of individuals within the production process there exists within the capitalist mode of production a generalised relation between labour and capital; it is this relation which constitutes the *class relation* between the capitalist class and the working class which is the fundamental social relation of capitalism. From this stem three further propositions. First, that class relations are not simply the aggregation of a multitude of employer-employee relations. Second, class membership or location of individuals is not to be derived simply from the occupations of individuals.[60] Third, it requires us to insist upon the relational character of the Marxist concept of class.

> The separate individuals form a class only in so far as they have to carry on a common battle against another class ... The class in its turn achieves an independent existence over against the individuals, so that the latter find their conditions of existence predestined, and hence have their position in life and their personal development assigned to them by their class, and become subsumed under it.[61]

Classes are, therefore, not things, but are sets of social relations, characterised by their general and pervasive existence and by the antagonistic character of the relation. As Braverman expresses it, the labour-capital relation 'creates a social relation, and as this relation is generalised throughout the productive process it creates social classes'.[62] An essentially similar point is made by Althusser when he argues that 'classes are function of the process of production as a whole'.[63]

It is necessary to stress that this line of argument does not imply that in any sense class relations precede, or even predate the technical relations of production. Rather it insists that the relation between worker and employer does not take on the character of a class relation unless it exists within the framework of the generalised existence of class relations.

Classes exist only at the level of class relations; or in other words, classes do not derive from the technical relations of production. This does not mean that class relations are independent or separate from production relations. Technical relations of production determine, firstly, the general form of the class-relation; thus the historical significance of factory production gives rise to the particular form of the capital-labour relation and specifically determines the character of class practices; it gives rise to 'the working class, a class always increasing in numbers, and disciplined, united, organised by the very mechanism of the process of capitalist production itself'.[64]

Capitalist social relations must therefore, be understood as an interactive combination of technical and class relations. It is the imposition of class relations upon the technical relations of production that reveals the distinctive character of the capitalist mode of appropriation of surplus-labour through the extraction of surplus-value (capitalist-worker class relations + commodity production).

The most important consequence of insisting that class relations exist at a level distinct from the technical relations of production is that it allows us to approach the part played by politics and ideology in the determination of classes. It is, however, important to note that this approach does depart not only from some of Marx's own formulations, but also from that advanced by Poulantzas, and also by Balibar. In *Capital*, Volume III, Marx in the course of a general formulation argues:

The specific economic form, in which unpaid surplus-labour is pumped out of direct producers, determines the relationship of rulers and ruled, *as it grows directly out of production itself* and, in turn, reacts upon it as a determining element. Upon this, however, is founded the entire formation of the economic community which grows up out of the production relations themselves, thereby its specific political form. It is always the direct relationship of the owners of the conditions of production to the direct producers – a relation always naturally corresponding to a definite stage in the development of the methods of labour and thereby its social productivity – which reveals the innermost secret, the hidden basis of the entire social structure.[65]

The analysis which I am suggesting cannot therefore rest upon textual authority alone. It is clear that there is a basic ambiguity, if not even a contradiction, within Marx which on the one hand asserts the primacy of the economic level, and on the other locates classes explicitly in terms of ideological and political relations.[66]

The political and ideological dimensions of class relations can be approached by means of an examination of one of Marx's better known formulations concerning class in *The Eighteenth Brumaire*.

In so far as millions of families live under economic conditions of existence that separate their mode of life, their interests and their culture from those of other classes, and put them in hostile opposition to the latter, they form a class. In so far as there is merely a local interconnection among these small-holding peasants, and the identity of their interests begets no community, no national bond and no political organisation among them, they do not form a class.[67]

This passage is not some Hegelian throw-back to a conception of class-for-itself. Rather it asserts that classes cannot be conceived as having an existence separate from the ideological and political levels. Classes therefore are not economic relations.

The economic level of the technical relations of production prescribe the parameters or outer boundaries of class structures. The identification of the working class is therefore not a matter of debate between alternative economic criteria; it cannot be reduced to a contest between 'productive labour' and 'wage labour' as the critical determinant of a class boundary. The economic level prescribes the possible extent or limit of class boundaries. It is in this context that it is possible to argue that a conception of the working class specified as wage-labourers and the non-owners of the means of production provides the *possible* or *potential* boundaries of the working class. Whether particular categories of workers, be they commercial workers or state employees, form part of the working class is not determined solely at the economic level. Thus when we are concerned with the class location of 'white collar workers', our analysis must embrace their changing role within the labour process, which as Braverman establishes can be expressed in terms of proletarianisation, but also in terms of their political and ideological practices, for example the extent and forms of trade union practice. But it is not simply that white collar unionism is the *result* of their changing position within the labour process. It is also necessary to insist that white collar unionism, as ideological and political practices, has its impact upon the labour process, producing new types of relations between employees and their employers and managers. The analysis of the class location of white collar workers can only be undertaken if it expressly embraces the interaction between the economic, political and ideological levels. Thus Braverman's study only undertakes one part of the study of the class location of this expanding sector of the labour-force in that he concentrates exclusively on changes in the labour process.

I have already argued that classes should not be conceived of as 'things', as fixed entities that can be identified solely at the level of economic relations. Classes only exist as sets of practices or activities, which constitute *class practices*, that is they give effect on the one hand to an antagonistic relation to other practices, and therefore to another class; and on the other hand, bring them into closer relations with the practices that determines the *class identification* of any section or category of the population.

Political and ideological practices have the effect of establishing the relation of the participants to classes. These practices can be conceived as 'linking' or 'tying' the participants to a class; and on the other hand of 'separating' or 'distancing' them from another class location. Thus if we return to the problem of technicians and managers, we can insist that it is not simply their function in the production process, as 'the function of capital', that determines their class position. Rather it is the political and ideological practices within which their function in the production process is carried out that is decisive. Hence the subjective orientation of such sections are important, not, as bourgeois sociologists would argue, because it determines their class location, but as evidence of the effects of politics and ideology. Hence if managers, for example, identify their interests with the owners of capital then this is the effect of political and ideological relations. These practices must be studied in their relation to the economic level; where their income is linked to company profits, for example, it will have the effect of reinforcing an ideological proximity to capital.

It is on the basis of this type of analysis that I would suggest that we are able to 'exclude' military and police personnel from the working class; we do not need to rely upon economic criteria. The example of the Portuguese army, and its various sections, illustrates a complex transition between a number of different class locations.

It is with respect to the differentiation *within* social classes that economic criteria play an important part in distinguishing between the different sections or strata of a class. Within a conception of the working class whose outer limits are prescribed by wage-labour and non-ownership of capital we can make use of the existence of different places within the labour process to distinguish between different strata; it is in this arena that the distinction between productive and unproductive labour will have its real significance. Yet it is also important to emphasise that fractions and strata must also be identified historically, that is as a result of concrete effects of the economic, political and ideological levels. I want to touch on two aspects of the differentiation of the working class that have some political significance. The first concerns the concept of the 'core' of the working class. This term is used to indicate that manual, productive factory workers occupy a special and central place within the working class, and constitute the most decisive sector of the class. The concept 'core' comes very close to Poulantzas's identification at the economic level of the working class. I want to suggest that the concept is not without problems, and to do so by posing the question: in what sense is the 'core' of the working class 'decisive'? There are two possible answers, one is economic and the other political. Economically it may be argued that the core of the working class is decisive because it produces surplus-value which is the central motive force of the capitalist mode of production. But if my previous argument is correct, that the production of surplus-value is increasingly undertaken by the 'collective labourer', and if it is also true that in the newer industries, such as electrical power production and petro-chemicals, a higher percentage of the work-force are technicians and other mental labourers, then it follows that the character of the economic core changes. Yet these newcomers to the economic core of the working class have relatively few of the characteristics of the factory proletariat.

The core of the working class can also be regarded as politically significant in that it is either actually, or potentially, the most class conscious section of the working class. Its political significance stems from the nature of factory and collective production which gives rise to the organisation of workers, especially in trade unions, and gives direct experience of capitalist exploitation.

If use is to be made of the concept of the 'core of the working class', it should not be confused with a notion of the 'traditional working class'. While historical experience of a section of workers plays a significant contribution to the nature and forms of their class practices (for example, the traditional high level of discipline of British miners in struggle), it cannot be regarded as part of the definition of the 'core'. Let me illustrate this point by reference to British dock-workers, who from the 1890s through to the late 1960s played a major part in the struggles of the working class; however, the economic changes and decline in the recent period has resulted in dockers playing a much less central role in the recent history of the British working class. Yet during the same period the increasing rate of unionisation of non-manual workers has resulted in them playing a much greater part in the labour movement, with some important signs of them bringing into the trade union movement a range of political and class issues, for example, those revolving around job-control, not automatically brought forward by the manual workers' unions. It is important, therefore, on both political and economic grounds to recognise that the 'core of the working class' is not fixed and static, but that its composition necessarily changes with the development that takes place within the capitalist mode of production. The development of revolutionary political strategy therefore requires a continuous and historically specific analysis of class formations and class relations.

These considerations lead on to a more general and concluding observation. The insistence that class identification cannot be posed in a definitional manner by selecting fixed criteria, and that classes can only exist through class practices, makes it possible to reintroduce Marx's distinction between class-in-itself and class-for-itself. These concepts have been much out of favour in recent Marxist debate as a consequence of the Hegelian context in which they were situated in Marx's thought. We may now be able to reinstate them.

If classes are to be identified through class practices, that is practices that express, on the one hand, the common experience of the class, and on the other, its opposition to another class, then it becomes necessary to distinguish between different levels of class practice. These levels can be indicated, not by reference to any preordained hierarchy which, for example, defines 'revolutionary class struggle' as being on a higher level than 'economic class struggle'. Rather, levels of class practice may be identified in so far as they give effect to realising the maximum potential involvement of different groups with the social relations of production as 'class forces'.

Higher levels of class practice will be indicated as those forms which give effect to the mobilisation of class practices which embrace, link and unite all wage-earners/non-owners of the means of production. These levels of class practice provide the content of Marx's concept class-for-itself. A class can only be said to exist as a class-for-itself when, through its class practices, it exercises a hegemonic influence over those that compose it; that is, it constitutes a unity in terms of practices which give effect to a unity of interests for its full potential dimension, embracing all wage earners. In so doing it separates itself as a class from the class to which it stands in opposition, the capitalist class.

REFERENCES

1. Similarly this was the primary focus of class analysis in the Chinese revolution.
2. Lenin, *Collected Works* III, 23–607.

3. Mao Tse-tung, *Selected Works* I, 13–22 and 23–59.
4. For example my article 'Class Structure in Britain Today' (*Marxism Today*, 1970) does precisely this under the disguise of the concept 'middle strata'; this has been a tendency widely shared on the British Left.
5. Programme of the Communist Party of Great Britain, 1968; it should be pointed out that this programme is currently being revised.
6. According to the calculation of Wright, applying Poulantzas's definition, the working class constitutes no more than 15 per cent of the population of the United States; Wright (1976), 23.
7. Poulantzas (1973), and (1975).
8. See for a very useful general critique of Poulantzas, Wright (1976), and also Carchedi (1975b).
9. Marx, *Preface to a Contribution to the Critique of Political Economy*, Marx and Engels (1969), I, 503.
10. Poulantzas (1975), 18.
11. Ibid., p. 19.
12. Ibid., p. 20.
13. For example, 'In so far as millions of families live under economic conditions of existence that separate their mode of life, their interests and their culture from those of other classes, and put them in hostile opposition to the latter, they form a class' (Marx, *The Eighteenth Brumaire of Louis Bonaparte*, Marx and Engels (1958), I, p. 334).
14. Marx and Engels (1958), I, pp. 43–4.
15. Note the formulation that Marx uses in the *Preface* of 1859: 'At a certain stage of their development, the material productive forces come in conflict with the existing relations of production, or – what is but a legal expression for the same thing – with the property relations within which they have been at work hitherto' (Marx and Engels (1969), I, pp. 503–4).
16. This thesis is presented in Poulantzas (1973), pp. 37–9; Poulantzas (1974), pp. 237–46, and developed in Poulantzas (1975), Introduction and Part III.
17. Poulantzas (1975), p. 20.
18. Ibid., p. 20.
19. Poulantzas (1973), p. 30.
20. Marx (1973), pp. 88–100.
21. Marx (1959), p. 856; (1972), p. 878; and later in the same chapter: 'Let us moreover consider the so-called distribution relations themselves. The wage presupposes wage-labour, and profit-capital. These definite forms of distribution thus presuppose definite social characteristics of production conditions, and definite social relations of production agents. The specific distribution relations are thus merely expressions of the specific historical production relations' (Marx (1959), p. 860; (1972), p. 882).
22. For a very helpful and comprehensive discussion see Gough (1972).
23. A rough guide to the quantitative implications can be gathered from the Department of Employment statistics. For March 1976, 43 per cent of employed population were employed in commercial employment, whereas only 41 per cent were employed in production industries; whilst no workers employed in the commercial sector can be productive labourers, not all those employed in production industries will be productive labourers, e.g. supervisors, managers, etc. (Department of Employment Gazette, September 1976).

24. Ian Gough's article referred to above ably brings out the ambiguities, and complexities.
25. Poulantzas (1975), p. 216; emphasis in original.
26. Marx (1969), I, p. 401. See also his examples of the actor and the clown (Marx (1969), I, p. 157), and the schoolteacher (Marx (1961), I, p. 509).
27. For completion of the example, it should be noted that the self-employed window-cleaner cannot be classified as either a productive or an unproductive labourer since, as Marx notes, 'their production does not fall under the capitalist mode of production' (Marx (1969), I, p. 407).
28. Ibid., p. 230.
29. Marx (1961), I, pp. 508–9; for an even more explicit statement of the theme, embracing managers, engineers and technicians, within the 'collective labourer', see Marx (1976), p. 1040.
30. Braverman (1974), p. 418.
31. Marx (1973), p. 705.
32. Ibid., p. 240.
33. Marx (1961), p. 509.
34. I hasten to add that this must not be taken to suggest that these objects of inquiry are not related, it is simply that they are different.
35. Wright (1976), pp. 15–16.
36. See, for example, Poulantzas (1973a), Chapter I; and Hindess (1976).
37. 'For the worker it is equally consoling that because of the growth in the net product, more spheres are opened up for unproductive workers, who live on his product and whose interest in his exploitation coincides more or less with that of the directly exploiting classes' (Marx (1969), II, p. 571); and again: 'The middle classes maintain themselves to an ever-increasing extent directly out of revenue, they are a burden weighing heavily on the working base' (Marx, ibid., p. 573).
38. Marx (1972), p. 294.
39. Marx (1969), I, p. 401.
40. Anderson (1976); I would wish to suggest that it would be preferable to identify the broad trend by its substantive content, which may be specified as the reaction against an economic determinist interpretation of Marxism, rather than by its geographical location.
41. Colletti, 'Bernstein and the Marxism of the Second International' in Colletti (1972).
42. See in particular the famous late letters of Engels to Bloch, Schmidt, Mehring and Starkenburg (Marx and Engels (1960), pp. 498–507, pp. 540–4, and pp. 548–61).
43. This should be contrasted with the work of both Carchedi and Wright in whose respective analyses, which have important similarities, class boundaries are not exclusively determined at the economic level; the boundaries at the three levels are not in direct correspondence, that is, are not simply superimposed upon each other.
44. Poulantzas (1973), p. 37.
45. Ibid., p. 37.
46. Ibid., p. 38.
47. Marx (1961), I, p. 508.
48. Gramsci (1971), pp. 5–23.
49. It will be noted that this criticism, although having something in common with that made by Wright, who argues that Poulantzas 'undermines the economic basis of the theory of class' (Wright, 1976, p. 19), should be distinguished from it; it is important to note that Poulantzas's use of ideological determinant of class goes

hand in hand with a pronounced economism which I have pointed to above.

50. Poulantzas (1975), p. 229; or what Carchedi calls 'the function of capital', (1975a), pp. 23–4.
51. Wright (1976), p. 20.
52. Lenin, *The Development of Capitalism in Russia, Collected Works*, vol. 3, pp. 62–3.
53. Althusser and Balibar (1970).
54. Hindess and Hirst (1975).
55. Poulantzas (1973a), pp. 58–70; and also in Carchedi (1975a).
56. Carchedi (1975a), pp. 5–6, although it should be noted that the distinction he draws differs somewhat from Poulantzas's usage.
57. It should be noted that Marx's concept of productive forces, in addition to its reference to the forms of technology, also includes 'living labour', that is the available, historically given level of skills and knowledge of the agents of production.
58. Marx (1961), p. 714.
59. See Marx's discussion of 'The So-Called Primitive Accumulation' in *Capital* I, and Hindess and Hirst (1975), Chapter 6.
60. One implication of this production concerns the question of the class location of 'housewives', that is women not participating directly in the process of capitalist production. It is not necessary to proceed by ascribing them to the same class as their husbands or fathers. Their location is determined by the necessary function of reproducing labour-power (not to be confused with biological reproduction) within the capitalist mode of production; the generalised form of this activity within capitalist society to date has been in the form of the individualised family unit within which women expend their necessary but 'unproductive' labour.
61. Marx and Engels (1964), p. 69.
62. Braverman (1974), p. 413; a slight reservation should be added about this formulation since it does carry the possible implication that class relations arise simply from the quantitative extension of the labour-capital relation.
63. Althusser and Balibar (1970), p. 267.
64. Marx (1961), p. 763.
65. Marx (1972), p. 791, my emphasis.
66. Barry Hindess also stresses this ambiguity within Marx; Hindess (1976).
67. Marx and Engels (1958), I, p. 334.

BIBLIOGRAPHY

Althusser and Balibar (1970), *Reading Capital*, New Left Books, London.

Anderson, Perry (1976), *Considerations on Western Marxism*, New Left Books, London.

Braverman, Harry (1974), *Labour and Monopoly Capitalism*, Monthly Review Press, New York.

Carchedi, G. (1975a), 'On the Economic Identification of the New Middle Class', *Economy and Society*, Vol. 4, no. 1, pp. 1–86.

Carchedi, G. (1975b), 'Reproduction of Social Classes at the Level of Production Relations', *Economy and Society*, Vol. 4, no. 4, pp. 361–417.

Colletti, Lucio (1972), *From Rousseau to Lenin: Studies in Ideology and Society*, New Left Books; London.

Dos Santos, Theotonio (1970), 'The Concept of Social Classes', *Science and Society*, Vol. 43, no. 2, pp. 166–93.

Giddens, Anthony (1973), *The Class Structure of the Advanced Societies*, Hutchinson, London.

Gough, Ian (1972), 'Marx's Theory of Productive and Unproductive Labour', *New Left Review*, 76, pp. 47–72.

Gramsci, Antonio (1971), *Prison Notebooks*, Lawrence and Wishart, London.

Hindess, Barry (1976), 'Marxist Theory and Marxist Politics', paper presented at Communist University VIII, July.

Hindess and Hirst (1975), *Pre-Capitalist Modes of Production*, Routledge and Kegan Paul, London.

Hunt, Alan (1970), 'Class Structure in Britain Today', *Marxism Today*, Vol. 14, no. 6, pp. 167–73.

Lenin (1960–1970), *Collected Works*, Lawrence and Wishart, London.

Marx, Karl (1959), *Capital* III, Foreign Languages Publishing House, Moscow.

Marx, Karl (1961), *Capital* I, Foreign Languages Publishing House, Moscow.

Marx, Karl (1969), *Theories of Surplus Value* (3 volumes), Lawrence and Wishart, London.

Marx, Karl (1972), *Capital* III, Lawrence and Wishart, London.

Marx, Karl (1973), *Grundrisse*, Penguin, London.

Marx, Karl (1976), 'The Results of the Immediate Process of Production'; appendix to *Capital* I, Penguin.

Marx and Engels (1958), *Marx–Engels Selected Works* (2 volumes), Foreign Languages Publishing House, Moscow.

Marx and Engels (1960), *Selected Correspondence*, Foreign Languages Publishing House, Moscow.

Marx and Engels (1964), *The German Ideology*, Foreign Languages Publishing House, Moscow.

Marx and Engels (1969), *Selected Works* (3 volumes), Progress Publishers, Moscow.

Mao Tse-tung (1967), *Selected Works* (4 volumes), Foreign Languages Publishing House, Peking.

Ollman, Bertell (1968), 'Marx's Use of "Class"', *American Journal of Sociology*, vol. 73, pp. 573–80.

Poulantzas, Nicos (1973), 'On Social Classes', *New Left Review*, 78, pp. 27–54.

Poulantzas, Nicos (1973a), *Political Power and Social Classes*, New Left Books, London.

Poulantzas, Nicos (1974), *Fascism and Dictatorship*, New Left Books, London.

Poulantzas, Nicos (1975), *Classes in Contemporary Capitalism*, New Left Books, London.

Wright (1976), 'Class Boundaries in Advanced Capitalist Societies', *New Left Review*, 98, pp. 3–41.

THE NEW PETTY BOURGEOISIE

Nicos Poulantzas

I want to focus my attention on the question of the 'new petty bourgeoisie' about which I have already written in *Classes in Contemporary Capitalism* (New Left Books, 1975). I want to respond to some of the criticisms that have been made of my position both at this conference and elsewhere.* It is important to note that the criticisms that have been levelled are not mutually consistent; for example, Alan Hunt has criticised me for adopting an economistic position, while Stuart Hall claims that I pay insufficient attention to the economic level.

The problem posed by the discussion of the new petty bourgeoisie is that of specifying the boundary of the working class. This is not simply a theoretical problem; it involves political questions of the greatest general importance concerning the role of the working class and of alliances in the transition to socialism. At the outset I should like to make clear what are the political alternatives that confront us. If the working class is defined as embracing all those that sell their labour power then we must be clear about the implications of such a definition. Without being too polemical I want to insist that this definition of the working class must be viewed in the context of its history in the working-class movement. This definition first emerged in classical Social Democracy, and has remained the major definition of the working class relied upon by Social Democracy. We can turn the problem around as much as we wish but the facts remain: the Social Democratic position has been one which has defined the working class as the class composed of individuals who are wage earners, in other words it is a conception of a 'wage-earning class'. This definition can be traced back to Bernstein and to Kautsky. The justification for this definition is presented in the following terms. The working class about

* It should be borne in mind that I did not have an opportunity to read the papers presented by Stuart Hall, Alan Hunt and Paul Hirst before the conference.

which Marx wrote was the 'industrial proletariat' but it is necessary to take account of the actual economic and social transformations that have occurred since that period. These changes make it necessary, it is argued, to recognise that the boundaries of the working class have also been changed. Whenever social-democrats seek to make use of Marxism, but at the same time to 'revise' it, they always appeal to changes in capitalism to justify their position. Thus Kautsky argued that because of the actual changes undergone by capitalism the working class is no longer the narrow class that Marx wrote about, and that it is now composed of the whole of the 'wage-earning class'. To define the working class as the whole of the 'wage-earning class' has the effect of reducing the class divisions in society to the division between rich and poor. The class characteristics of the working class become nothing more than the economically poor citizens; class becomes simply a matter of inequality.

The major aspect of the problem to which I wish to draw attention concerns the problem of alliances and the hegemony of the working class in the transition to socialism. This is, as Alan Hunt has made clear, and here I agree with him, the main problem. The main problem is what type of hegemony must the working class achieve in order to achieve the transition to socialism? But we need to examine what the consequences are of adopting the 'broad' definition of the working class? To adopt the broad definition abolishes the problem of alliances; the problem does not exist any more because everyone has become a worker. The whole population with the exception of a very small minority are wage earners. As a consequence the working class no longer has to play a role of principled leadership over the other classes, because all other classes have been subsumed within the working class. It is in this respect that the major difference is to be found between the Marxist theory of the party, not only that of Lenin, but also of Gramsci, and the social democratic type of theory which is based on this conception of the large wage-earning class.

To turn to the second problem. Because I am not familiar in detail with the positions of the British Communist Party on this problem, I will concentrate on those adopted by the French and the Italian Communist Parties. These Communist Parties give a relatively restricted definition of the working class, in the sense that they define its limitations as prescribed by immediately or directly productive labour. There are some variations of detail that distinguish the positions of these Parties. They do differ as to the precise location of the limits of the working class; for example, the main difference concerns the question of technicians. They do, for example, exhibit somewhat distinct positions concerning the extent to which technicians are to be regarded as being part of the working class, but it is not a fundamental problem for them, since their theoretical positions exclude from the working class most of the salaried non-productive workers. From this point of view their position differs from the one put forward by Alan Hunt.

There is a further important problem associated with the definition of the working class adopted by the French Communist Party. If the non-productive wage-labourers (whom I will call for convenience 'salaried workers') are excluded from the working class, then it is necessary to determine their class location. The French Communist Party (PCF) does not speak of them as a class, rather it designates them as an 'intermediate strata'. I believe this to be an incorrect position, and here I agree with Alan Hunt, that it is false to imagine that there can exist 'strata' that are *outside* classes and the class structure, but which nevertheless are regarded as taking part in class struggle. Strata are designations of differentiations *within* classes, not categories that can exist outside classes. While Alan Hunt goes on to argue that these sections or 'strata' form part of the working class, I have argued that they belong to a specific class, namely the 'new petty bourgeoisie'.

Why have I argued that the new petty bourgeoisie constitutes a separate class? I want, in particular, to stress the political implications of my position. Even if we do not speak of a salaried class but of an intermediate strata, there is always the danger that we will not see clearly the central problem of revolutionary strategy, which is precisely the problem of the hegemony of the working class within the popular alliance in the transition to socialism.

What difference does it make if we regard salaried workers as an intermediate strata or as a specific class? The definite characteristic of strata, in comparison to classes, is that strata do not have specific and relatively autonomous class interests. This means that even if we exclude salaried workers from the working class we nevertheless see them as being automatically polarised towards the working class; and we therefore treat them as if they do not have specific interests of their own. Whereas if we see them as a specific class, distinct from the working class, we must give proper recognition and attention to their specific and distinctive class interests. So the problem of the hegemony of the working class presents itself as exactly how to organise the people, the popular alliance. This popular alliance is made up of *different* classes with specific class interests. If this was not the case the problem would be reduced to an extremely simple one.

Salaried non-productive workers have a specific class membership. Even if we recognise that as a consequence of the transformations of contemporary capitalism they are objectively polarised towards the working class; it is nevertheless important that we understand that this is never an automatic or inevitable process. This is true in two senses; first, that they must be won to an alliance with the working class, and in the second sense, even when they have been won, they can be lost as allies and they can turn to the other side. This is what happened in Allende's Chile and also in Portugal. If these salaried non-productive workers can shift from an alliance with the working class to an alliance with the bourgeoisie it is precisely because they are *not* automatically polarised towards the working class. This is not because they do not have specific class interests, but because they have a very dubious class specificity.

Now, one or two theoretical remarks about this conception of the intermediate salaried strata. First of all, is it not possible to speak of salaried strata as not having class membership? It points to one of the specific characteristics of Marx's class theory as distinct from other class theories. All bourgeois sociologists speak of classes nowadays, but classes for them are only particular divisions within a more general social statification in which we find not only classes, but also elites (in the political sphere), status groups, etc. Of course, Marxism recognises the existence of fractions, and specific categories of classes, but all those are fractions *of classes*. For example, the commercial bourgeoisie is a fraction of the bourgeoisie, and the labour aristocracy is a specific fraction of the working class itself. In Marxism we cannot admit to the existence of strata, fractions, and significant groupings outside of classes. Nor could one say that, as a result of the development of the mode of production (that is of the pure mode of production, which has two classes, the bourgeoisie and the working class), we would find a tendency within the social formation itself for all the individuals, all the agents, to become part either of the bourgeoisie or of the working class.

Such a position is absolutely false because it presupposes that the mode of production is an abstract concept, whereas 'social formation' is a non-abstract concept. A distinction between abstract and non-abstract concepts does not exist. The concept of 'dog' does not bark. All concepts are abstract to a greater or lesser degree. The distinction between the concepts 'social formation' and 'mode of production' revolves around the nature of the object. Mode of production is an abstract formal object and social formation a concrete real object. So this would presuppose that modes of production exist and reproduce themselves as such, and that social formations are nothing other than a geographical topographical place where modes of production, in their abstract reproduction, concretise themselves. So the pure mode of production, the capitalist mode of production (bourgeoisie and working class) reproducing itself in the abstract, would finish by 'revealing itself' like Christ, triumphal in the social formation where finally we would have only bourgeois and proletarian classes.

This position is false because as Lenin has shown in *The Development of Capitalism in Russia* the distinction between modes of production and social formations does not have to do with interpretation of Marx, 'young' and 'old Marx', or with the status of the *Communist Manifesto*, it concerns the texts of Lenin, and also the nature of imperialism. One cannot understand imperialism without the distinction between modes of production and social formation. It is not possible to deduce imperialism from the capitalist mode of production itself. Imperialism is a necessary effect of the reproduction and the existence of the mode of production in concrete social formations. Unequal development is not an effect of the simple concretisation of the capitalist mode of production conceived as an effect in reality, which develops towards imperialism; rather it is a constitutive element of imperialism itself. For this reason the dual conception of society cannot be accepted.

Having developed these theoretical and political points, I would like to discuss the major propositions which I have advanced in my text *Classes in Contemporary Capitalism*. These propositions are as follows: (i) that there exists a specific class situation of the salaried non-productive workers which I have called the 'new petty bourgeoisie'; (ii) that there are transformations in the reproduction of capitalism which have to do with extensions of the limits of the working class, but that nevertheless those transformations do not change the specific class situations of the new petty bourgeoisie; (iii) that these transformations affect the new petty bourgeoisie in the sense that it is increasingly objectively polarised towards the working class as a specific class, but because the new petty bourgeoisie has a specific class situation this objective polarisation does not concern the whole of the class to the same extent. It rather concerns certain fractions of the new petty bourgeoisie which constitute a large majority of it.

We now need to consider if it would be a solution to the problem if one could speak of 'contradictory class locations'? I want to consider the thesis advanced by Erik Wright in his article 'Class Boundaries in Advanced Capitalist Societies' (*New Left Review*, 98). Can we resolve the theoretical problem by saying that some agents have a contradictory class location? This implies that these agents can occupy different and changing class locations; it suggests that they can occupy a vacuum, a no-man's-land between the bourgeoisie and the working class.

We can approach this theoretical problem by focusing upon the nature of supervision within the capitalist process of production. When Marx spoke about the labour of supervision and direction of the labour process he insisted upon the double nature of this labour. Indeed he always used the same expression, saying that on the one hand as long as supervisory labour is necessary to every labour-process as such, to production in general, then in this sense it is part of productive labour; and, on the other hand, that as long as it concerns the realisation of surplus-value, and not the production of it, it constitutes a political control over the working class and, therefore, is not productive labour. I think that this kind of reasoning has to do with what Marx says, very clearly, in those passages in *Capital* in which he discusses 'production in general' and 'production as such', but Marx always says that production in general never exists in reality. The only thing that exists is a production process under given relations of production and within a given class struggle. Classes do not exist at first as such, and then enter into class struggle. Classes exist only as long as they are in struggle with one another. Taking account of these two arguments, I think it is impossible to say that some agents can have, in a given social formation and under given social relations, and in a definite class struggle, contradictory class locations. Marx, after all, made an important statement, in the context of this double nature of the labour-process, about the work of the capitalist himself; he says that, for as long as capitalist activity concerns the direction and co-ordination necessary for every labour-process and production as such, one can say that the capitalist performs productive labour. But can we, therefore, say that the capitalist has a contradictory class location, that he is both 'worker' and 'capitalist'? It would be a perfect absurdity. This set of arguments indicates the general nature of my response to Wright's article.

It has been pointed out that I have a rather limited and restricted definition of the working class. I want now to consider the argument, used by both Wright and Hunt, who draw attention to the fact that if we make use of the Marxist definition of class which I have proposed and apply it to the United States we find that the working class constitutes less than 20 per cent of the population. Let us examine this argument. First, I think that we cannot speak of classes in contemporary capitalism referring only to each particular social formation; we must always take into account the imperialist context. So the question of the working class, and the work-force that is subject to American capital has not only to do with the domestic working class. We must recognise that the working class which works for American capital includes also those who work, for example, for American firms in Latin America. So the question of the numerical size of the working class, especially when we speak of imperialist countries, must not only be seen in a national, but in a more imperialist context.

Secondly, the issues under discussion raise the very important problem of the transition to socialism, and also the problem of the hegemony of the working class. I want to insist that this cannot be reduced simply to a numerical problem; it is a political problem. It is not by gaining 5 per cent that the political task of winning a majority of the people for the transition to socialism is going to be achieved by the working class.

Third, there is a real problem which revolves around the fact that in the reproduction of capitalism there is a tendency towards a restriction of the importance of the working class in the production process in the imperialist countries, which is associated with the primacy of dead labour over living labour, and has to do with relative surplus value. It is not my intention to deny any of these facts. To do so would not take us anywhere; but I do not think that this is the important problem. The important problem is the political one. In my analysis of the new petty bourgeoisie, which I have set out here briefly, I began of course with the economic criterion, the distinction between productive and unproductive labour. I simply say somewhat dogmatically that things are perfectly clear for Marx. In *Capital* the one exception concerns the problem of technicians. It revolves around relative surplus value, as a counter-tendency to the falling rate of profit, with productivity of labour, and with exploitation mainly through relative surplus labour, and with technological innovations. There is this problem in Marx, but I do not think that there is a problem with the other non-productive workers, workers in the service and commercial sectors, workers involved with circulation, realisation or collection of surplus value. In a very clear way, although Marx might be wrong, he says, in particular in many passages in *Capital*, that commerical employees cannot be conceived as productive labourers. For these purposes it makes little difference if we adopt the criterion of the material or non-material production. If the workers in the commercial sphere are not considered by Marx to perform productive labour, it is not because they do not perform material production; in some instances they do, but it is because they depend on commercial capital and the only capital that produces surplus-value is productive capital. I have demonstrated that this involves the basic elements of Marx's theory of value, and this is why I have based my argument upon it.

I want to insist, nevertheless, that when I speak of productive and unproductive labour, I have tried to show that this is not a technical characteristic of this or that type of labour, but that it has to do with the relations of production, that is with the forms of exploitation. Productive labour in different modes of production is nothing but that labour which is exploited through the specific type of exploitation that characterises that mode of production – for example, the production of surplus value in the capitalist mode of production. It does not mean that salaried unproductive workers are not exploited – they are – which is of course extremely important, but not in the specific fashion that constitutes the production of surplus value.

Now leaving aside the problem concerning technicians in Marx's treatment, I have tried to show concretely what it means to say that the definition of social classes cannot be limited exclusively to the economic sphere, and that we must take into account politics and ideology. This has been a fundamental thesis advanced in *Political Power and Social Classes*. I want, therefore, to demonstrate why I needed those political and ideological elements. I needed them because, even if the criterion of productive and unproductive labour is sufficient to exclude unproductive workers from the working class it is not adequate, because it is a negative criterion. It tells us what they are not; that they are not part of the bourgeoisie, in that they do not have either the juridical or the economic ownership of the means of production. Further, it demonstrates that they are not part of the working class. But this economic criterion in itself is not sufficient to tell us to which class they belong. It is in this context that the political and the ideological criteria are important. I want to state briefly what I mean by them, and to indicate why this position has nothing to do with the distinction between 'class in itself' and 'class for itself'.

I agree with Alan Hunt that the economic (the relations of production and of exploitation) is not sufficient in order to define positively the class determination of unproductive salaried workers, and that we must always take into account the political and ideological elements of the social division of labour. To do this I made a distinction between 'structural class determination', which has to do with economic, political and ideological elements, in which the economic level always has the determining role, and 'class position' in a specific conjuncture of class struggle. Political and ideological elements do not only concern the class position in a specific conjuncture. It is very common to find that class in itself – structural class determination – is thought of only at the economic level, and then politics and ideology are introduced in the process of the class struggle in a conjuncture, 'class for itself'.

From the moment that we speak of the structural existence of classes, political and ideological elements are present. This means those political and ideological elements are not to be identified simply with an autonomous political revolutionary organisation of the working class, or with a revolutionary ideology. Even when the working class does not have this autonomous political organisation – the Communist Party – and does not have revolutionary ideology, it necessarily occupies specific places, not only in the economic sphere, but also in the ideological and political sphere.

This means that we can speak of specific ideological elements of the working class even if this working class does not have a revolutionary ideology and is dominated by bourgeois ideology. The working class always exists in class struggle through specific practices even when no revolutionary organisation exists. There always exists an ideology which makes the working class distinct from the bourgeois class. The United States, for example, is a classic example of a country with a working class without a revolutionary ideology and without an autonomous revolutionary party, or mass party. But this does not mean that the working class exists only at the economic level. The working class has an autonomous discourse, or at least elements of an autonomous discourse, which Lenin called 'class instinct', which bursts through the envelope that is the domination of borgeois ideology.

Autonomous political organisation and the revolutionary ideology of the working class have to do with the class position in the conjuncture. They are concerned with the making of the working class as a 'social force', which determines the possibility of the working class making a transition to socialism, that is to make social revolution. So the problem presents itself as to how to locate the political and ideological elements in the structural determination of a class, even if those elements are not the ones traditionally regarded as constituting the 'class for itself'. I have tried to show what these political and ideological elements are in the concrete analysis of the new petty bourgeoisie, and that they stem from its specific charactistics, not only with respect to productive and unproductive labour, but also from its position in the whole of the social division of labour.

I have tried to analyse the implications of the division between manual and mental labour. The division between manual and mental labour is not a physiological or biological division between those who work with their hands and those who work with their brains. It has to do with the social conditions under which the division between mental and manual labour exists, which as Gramsci pointed out, concern the whole series of rituals, 'know how', and symbols. Through this analysis we can define the division between manual and mental labour as being the concrete manifestation of the political and ideological elements in the structural determination of class.

I have tried to show why the new petty bourgeoisie, even its lower strata, are placed on the side of mental labour in the complex political-ideological division that distinguishes this mental labour from the manual labour performed by the working class. This does not mean that the working class works only with its hands, and the new petty bourgeoisie only with its brain. These divisions between productive and unproductive labour, and between manual and mental labour are tendential divisions. They are not models to be used to determine the position within the class structure of every individual agent; on the contrary it is concerned with the whole process of class struggle.

The Marxist concept of class is not a statistical category. It is necessary to show concretely, taking account of the detailed division of labour and of skill in the labour process, why even the lower strata of the new petty bourgeoisie are on the side of intellectual or mental labour with respect to their relations with the working class. Gramsci demonstrated in a concrete way that all public servants, all the servants of the state, from head to toe, must be considered as intellectuals in the general sense. I have taken other characteristics, in particular the bureaucratisation of labour in the organisation of the labour process of unproductive workers in order to show the significance of the distribution of authority. It is these elements, the political and ideological elements, which determine the class position of the new petty bourgeoisie. The new petty bourgeoisie interiorises the social division of labour imposed by the bourgeoisie throughout the whole of the society. Each level of the new petty bourgeoisie exercises specific authority and ideological domination over the working class, which takes on particular characteristics within the factory division of labour, since the workers do not exert any kind of authority or ideological dominance over other workers, for example, over unskilled workers, that has even remotely the same characteristics as that exercised by the different levels of the new petty bourgeoisie over the working class. These are the political and ideological elements in the social division of labour that I have taken to show the class specificity of the new petty bourgeoisie. It is important to stress that these are elements that have nothing to do with the so-called 'class for itself'.

Finally I have tried to show the way in which the transformation of contemporary capitalism operates in such a way as to produce an objective polarisation of important fractions of the new petty bourgeoisie towards the working class. I have tried to show that the division of manual and mental labour, as long as it has to do with the reproduction of political and ideological elements, reproduces itself within mental labour on the one hand, and within manual labour on the other. Some fractions of the new petty bourgeoisie, even if they are orienting themselves towards the working class, are also orienting themselves in relation to other fractions of the new petty bourgeoisie. The objective conditions for polarisation become greater as we approach the barrier of manual labour, with the repetitive type of labour performed by commercial employees and office workers. The objective possibilities exist for an alliance of the working class with certain fractions of the new petty bourgeoisie, and for the realisation of the hegemony of the working class. But it must clearly be understood that because they are members of another class, the new petty bourgeoisie, they must be *won* by the working class. But this does not occur automatically; the new petty bourgeoisie does not automatically adopt the class position of the working class. Even more important: it must be understood that when the working class has won them they can also be lost again.

ECONOMIC CLASSES AND POLITICS

Paul Hirst

This paper is concerned with the problem of the relationship between classes of economic agents and political institutions, practices and ideologies. For vulgar Marxism this relationship is unproblematic: political structures and events are more or less directly determined by the economic structure. The political is conceived as an expression in social struggles of economic developments. The nature and outcome of these political struggles is determined 'in advance' by the development of the forces of production. In general there can be no long-run discrepancy between the economic position of agents and their political position. For example, ruling class ideologies may delude sections of the working class, but in the long run the economically determined development of the struggle will polarise the class forces and bring the mass of the workers to 'see' their class interests and position.

The problem with this economistic Marxism is that when we turn to confront the dominant political issues and struggles of the day, 'classes', categories of economic agents, are not directly present in them. We encounter state apparatuses, parties (some of which claim a class identification, others not), campaign organisations (Child Poverty Action Group, Stop the '70 Tour, etc.), trade union and employers' organisations, bodies of armed men, demonstrations, riotous mobs, etc., but never *classes*. Only the naïve will reply that the Confederation of British Industries (CBI) *is* the capitalist class or that the trade unions *are* the working class — at best these institutions could be said to 'represent' these classes more or less adequately. How adequately depends on one's politics. To some businessmen Campbell Adamson was a dangerous radical, and Sir Frederick Catherwood no better than a socialist. To many leftists the trade unions are an apparatus of capitalist control designed to hobble shop-floor militancy. So much for the *forces* acting in the political, what about the *issues* at stake? Just as classes are not political organisations, so political struggles do not occur in the form of direct contests between classes for political hegemony, contests in which the issue is the nature of the social relations of production: capitalism versus socialism. Lenin scathingly derided the ultra-left economism which believed in such a contest of classes and social systems:

To imagine that social revolution is *conceivable* without revolts by small nations in the colonies and in Europe, without revolutionary outbursts by a section of the petty bourgeoisie *with all its prejudices*, without a movement of the politically non-conscious proletarian or semi-proletarian masses against oppression by landowners, the church and the monarchy, against national oppression, etc. – to imagine all this is to *repudiate social revolution.* So one army lines up in one place and says, 'We are for socialism', and another, somewhere else and says, 'We are for imperialism', and that will be a social revolution! . . . . whoever expects a 'pure' social revolution will *never* live to see it (*The Discussion on Self-Determination Summed Up, Collected Works,* vol. 22, pp. 355–6).

The autocracy and the war created the balances of political forces which made the February and October revolutions in Russia possible and they defined the issues. The Bolshevik Party, a socialist party, entered a revolutionary coup d'état with the slogan, *'peace, land, bread'*. In China there was no 'proletarian revolution' separate from and parallel to the struggle for national liberation.

These all-too-familiar examples indicate what is at stake in this question of economism – the recognition of the dominant political issues and the forces active in respect of them. Great Marxist leaders like Lenin and Mao Tse-tung have confronted this specificity of political struggles and forces and came to terms with it – *in political practice.* Economistic Marxism has remained, however, the dominant basic form of Marxist theory. I can imagine those who would say that my sketch of economistic Marxism at the beginning is a fiction and that no serious Marxist has ever taken that position. On the contrary, that is the position which the vast majority of serious Marxists have taken and still, by default, do take. Neither Lenin nor Mao Tse-tung, nor Gramsci nor any other leading Communist political leader ever criticised these basic economistic positions as such or provided a theoretical alternative to them.

Two crucial issues are at stake here:

(i) the identification of political forces – Lenin made it absolutely clear on numerous occasions that one could not read-off from the economic situations of the classes the balance of political forces. In *The Agrarian Programme of Social Democracy in the First Russian Revolution* Lenin proceeds to assess the balance of class forces through political organisations, their programmes and their ideologies. He – quite inevitably, engaged as he was in political struggle – fails to raise any general questions about this *reverse order of reading*. Yet, this reverse order rests on a necessary discrepancy between economic relations and political forces.

(ii) the identification of political issues – despite the theory of imperialism, of 'uneven development', etc., there is no necessary general connection presented in the work of Lenin and Mao between the form of the national political crisis and the conditions of capitalist development in a country. Each national situation must be appraised in its specificity, no 'mechanical application' of Leninism can enable one to read in the political situation the key crises and planes of fracture.

Louis Althusser attempted to confront this situation in his essay 'Contradiction and Over-Determination'. He recognised the discrepancy between Lenin's practice and the orthodox economistic conceptions of Marxism. He sought to eradicate this discrepancy by making the basic concepts of Marxist theory ('the dialectic') adequate to Lenin's practice. He conceived this not as a revision of Marxism but as a restoration of the Marxist dialectic ever-present since Marx's break with Hegel and yet theoretically unreflected, lacking the categories appropriate to its specificity. This led Althusser into the Marx–Hegel relation, into differentiating the Marxist and the Hegelian conceptions of the social totality and of its development. Economistic Marxism represented an essentialist conception of totality; a totality governed by an expressive causality in which the essence is manifest and co-present in its phenomena. Althusser conceived the Marxist totality as a complex hierarchy of relatively autonomous 'levels'. This hierarchy was determined 'in the last instance' by the economic in that it was the economic, as the global structure of the mode of production, which determined the 'place' of each of the instances in the hierarchy (including the economic level itself – represented as an instance).

The concept of 'relative autonomy' was the basic form in which Althusser attempted to give theoretical recognition to the specificity of political forces and issues. This concept of 'relative autonomy' involves three basic elements:

(i)   the political level is 'relatively' autonomous in that it exists within limits set by the global structure of the mode of production – it exists *as an instance* in order to represent the conditions of class society and its place in the hierarchy of instances, whether dominant or subordinate, is assigned to it by the structure of the mode of production.

(ii) the political level *represents* the social classes which exist at the economic level, this representation is conceived as being something more than simple reflection or expression.

(iii) it follows that there must be a necessary discrepancy between the classes at the level of the economic and the forces represented in politics – this is due to the action of the means of representation (if there were no such discrepancy then the relation of the economic and the political would again be the rejected one of expression or reflection).

This position of Althusser's has been taken up in successive studies by Nicos Poulantzas. Both Althusser and Poulantzas attempt the same general solution to the problem of the specificity of political forces and issues. To restate the problem. Economistic Marxism resolves the question of the nature of the political struggles and the forces active in them into the level of development of the forces of production:

(i)   political forces and class forces ultimately correspond along the planes of polarisation established by the contradiction between the forces and relations of production;

(ii) political issues ultimately correspond to this polarisation of class forces.

Marxist political leaders and thinkers like Lenin and Mao Tse-tung rejected this conception in political practice since it led to the negation or mis-recognition of the issues at stake and the forces active in them. The effect of their intervention was to make the identification of political issues and forces a matter of accurately reading the 'current situation' or 'the concrete conjuncture'.

Althusser attempted to resolve this impasse by theorising this rejection of economism. The results of the failure of his own solution have been to return us to the status quo ante, but with the recognition that this status quo is untenable.

I. The theory of 'relative autonomy' derived from the theory of the complex totality governed by structural causality (fully elaborated in *Reading Capital* but present also in the two main studies in *For Marx*). This theory explained the autonomy of the political level and its limits as a function of the global structure of the mode of production. Structural causality is the causality of a self-reproducing eternity. In the causality of economistic Marxism a critical polarisation of class forces is a necessary outcome. In the eternity classes are assigned places in the economic structure and politics is assigned a role in the totality. There can be no political crises in this eternity, since a crisis, and the issues and forces active in it, refers us to some definite state of affairs. Thus to the theory of the structure of modes of production Althusser adds the necessity of reference to specific social formations and to definite 'current situations' or 'concrete conjunctures' in them. These conjunctures are in essence untheorised. Both economism and Althusserianism lead paradoxically to the same effect. Economism abolishes the specificity of political issues and forces in a necessary general crisis. Structural causality excludes by definition reference to specific states of affairs – political issues and forces cannot be conceived at this level. Althusser's 'current situations' are no more adequately theorised than were Lenin's.

II. The concept of 'relative autonomy' depends crucially on the concept of 'representation'. I have discussed this problem at length in a recent paper ('Althusser and the Theory of Ideology' in *Economy and Society*, vol. 5, no. 4) and so I will be brief here. The concept of 'relative autonomy' is inherently unstable – it is (to use a term from one of

Althusser's earliest works) a 'practical concept', an attempt to register and to overcome a difficulty. If the concept of 'representation' means anything more than 'reflection' or 'expression', with qualifications, then the notion of *relative* autonomy of the political *vis-à-vis* economic classes becomes problematic. What is at stake is not the autonomy but its relativity. The forces *represented* in politics are constituted by definite *means of representation* (parties, organisations, ideologies, programmes, etc.). These means must affect what it is that they 'represent'. These means constitute definite political forces. To say these forces *stand for* certain economic classes is either simply to accept the *claims* of a party, organisation or apparatus to represent a certain class, or, to argue that the party's programme and actions somehow correspond with the 'interests' of that class. Membership or allegiance – the sociological composition of the constituency of a party, the class backgrounds of the personnel of an apparatus – can furnish no proof that the apparatus or the party *represents* a class. It can always be argued that these personnel and adherents are unrepresentative or deluded. Furthermore, the theory of economic classes is not so precise as to permit such an identification of personnel or adherents. The inconclusive and interminable debates on productive and unproductive labour and on the nature of the 'middle strata' testify to this. But these 'interests' are not given independently of the means of representation: they do not exist in themselves. If one believes they do then one returns to economism. The economic situation of a class produces class 'experience' and the long run course of economic development gives that experience a necessary form. The status of class 'interests' if one rejects economism becomes problematic. Yet it is only with reference to 'interests' that one can discuss the question of the 'representivity' of political forces with respect to economic classes.

It follows that the notion of *relative* autonomy is untenable. Once any degree of autonomous action is accorded to political forces as means of representation *vis-à-vis* classes of economic agents, then there is no necessary correspondence between the forces that appear in the political (and what they 'represent') and economic classes. It is not simply a question of discrepancy (the political means 'represent' the class more or less accurately) but of necessary non-correspondence. One cannot, despite Lenin, 'read back' – measuring the political forces against what they are supposed to represent. That is to conceive the represented as external to, as the autonomously existent measure of, its means of representation. Classes do not have given 'interests', apparent independently of definite parties, ideologies, etc., and against which these parties, ideologies, etc., can be measured. What the means of representation 'represent' does not exist outside the process of representation. The 'represented' carries no sign, no means of recognition, other than that constituted by its means of representation. The issues, the ideologies the classes specified within the political arena are constituted there – one cannot read back beyond it to some essential arena of class struggle beyond politics. This is what is meant by non-correspondence.

When one makes a claim for or challenges the 'representivity' of a political organisation one is making a political appraisal, relative to some ideology and some model of organisation. To say that the Labour Party does not 'represent' the working class or betrays its 'interests' is to compare it with other and preferred means of 'representation' (a rank-and-file movement, the Communist Party, etc.) and to assign it this status relative to an ideology (syndicalism, Marxist theory of social democracy, etc.). It is to remain within politics, to make a critical political point in a certain way. It is to say that the Labour Party is not a revolutionary socialist party.

Either, economism, or the non-correspondence of political forces and economic classes – that is the choice which faces Marxism. Accepting non-correspondence means abandoning the evaluation of political forces in terms of correspondence, and evaluating them instead relative to one's conception of socialist organisation and ideology, and relative to one's estimation of the dominant political issues. Getting rid of sociologistic reductions and searching for 'class bases' will force Marxists to clarify their conception of what a socialist movement is (the standard of evaluation of the political forces) and what the current crucial struggles are (the 'sides' in these struggles will then tell us who our allies are).

The 'relative autonomy' of the political level avoids this choice only in words. Analyses conducted under the aegis of this concept constantly relapse into economism. Either, the state or the political party becomes a Machiavellian master-subject which gives recognition to and serves the interests of economic classes, or, the state and the political merely articulate class interests and forces which exist already formed at the level of the economic. This collapse into a more or less sophisticated economism is evident in Althusser's paper 'Ideology and Ideological State Apparatuses' (ISAs) (which I have criticised in the paper mentioned above and will not discuss here) and in Poulantzas' book *Classes in Contemporary Capitalism*.* It is this latter work which we will consider here.

Poulantzas, commendably, unlike many sociological and Marxist discussions of class, attempts to make his text of contemporary political relevance. His analyses are interventions in the debates on the EEC, state monopoly capitalism and the 'anti-monopoly alliance', and the question of the 'middle strata'. They amount to a sustained attack on the positions of the French Communist Party (PCF). In this critique he bases his position on the formation, development and polarisation of class forces *at the level of the economic*. He qualifies his analysis throughout by insisting from the very beginning that the social determination of classes and their political positions are distinct and irreducible. Analysis at the level of the economic (changes in balance of economic importance between 'fractions' of capital, for example) cannot, therefore, explain the balance of political forces or the political 'positions' of social classes at any given point. Poulantzas concludes with a political disclaimer: his positions on politics 'are simply intended to locate the problem and cannot claim to provide a solution to the question: 'what is to be done, and how?'" (Poulantzas, p. 335). This is a task of the revolutionary movement as a whole and depends on 'precise investigations' (p. 336).

It follows from this:

(i) that even if Poulantzas's attack on the economic analysis upon which the PCF's strategy is supposed to be founded was justified it would not follow that the PCF's *strategy* was incorrect in the current situation given the actual political positions of the social classes.

(ii) that concrete analysis is not merely a matter of adding 'precise investigations' to Poulantzas's general formulations, since, if the political positions of social classes can differ from their class determinations this difference must have conditions of existence.

* Translated by David Fernback (New Left Books, 1975).

These conditions are unknown and uninvestigated by Poulantzas. They could therefore render his analysis *redundant* for politics.

Poulantzas ends up in exactly the hiatus we have noted above, a hiatus which characterises both economistic and anti-economistic class analysis: the issues and the forces at stake in politics escape class analysis, they remain unknown and undetermined outside its categories, and yet class analysis pretends to define the conditions which determine these issues and forces.

In this paper I will attempt to show:

(i) that Poulantzas's class determination/class position distinction is incoherent and unstable, that it does not avoid the effect of economism (section A).

(ii) that his conception of the 'middle strata' requires him to differentiate the 'new petty bourgeoisie' from the working class on the basis of dubious extensions of Marx's concepts of productive and unproductive labour; Poulantzas is using economic distinctions to 'save' social and political differences between occupational categories, to exclude certain groups from the working class (section B).

(iii) Poulantzas's concept of 'class determination' leads to a generalisation and indefinition of his conception of the 'political' such that the state and state power becomes an all-pervasive social force and the specificity of political apparatuses is lost – this has serious political/strategic consequences (section C).

A. CLASS DETERMINATION, CLASS POSITION AND ECONOMISM

Poulantzas rejects the notion that social classes are defined purely at the level of the economic: '. . . a social class is defined by its place in the ensemble of social practices, i.e. by its place in the social division of labour as a whole. This includes political and ideological relations' (p. 14). The social division of labour has political, ideological and economic components. The social division of labour defines the places of classes in its structure. Classes are globally determined by the combined structure of the 'instances' which form a definite social division of labour. The social division of labour and the classes it defines are an effect of the social totality itself: 'Social class, in this sense, is a concept which denotes the effects of the structure within the social division of labour (social relations and social practices)' (p. 14). *Class determination therefore is equivalent to structural determination.*

However, Poulantzas follows this by saying: 'Classes exist only in the class struggle' (ibid.). Class determination=structural determination. Classes, however, exist only in struggle. Poulantzas follows this remark with a qualification '. . . class determination must not be reduced, in a voluntarist fashion to class position' (pp. 14–15, cf. p. 201). Class struggle must be the struggle of *class positions*. It follows that class determination, structural determination, cannot be reduced to the class struggle.

What then is the relation between class determination and class practice? Poulantzas says: 'A social class, or a fraction or stratum of a class, may take up a class position that does not correspond to its interests, which are defined by the class determination that fixes the horizon of the class's struggle' (p. 15). We know that class determination and class position can differ and that class determination must not be reduced to class position. Class determination constitutes the 'interests' of a class, these 'interests' serve to measure whether or not a given class position diverges from the class's structural determination. Class determination also 'fixes the horizon' of a class's struggle, that is, structural determination sets limits to the possible class positions. Class position is, therefore, the possible degree of concrete difference from the 'interests' of a class. It is an effect of specific conditions which modify the general structural determination but within the limits of the structure. The conjuncture and the class struggle modify the general class determinations. But what are the conditions of existence of those modifications? Where does the 'concrete' which effects this modification come from? The structure cannot be abstract if it is to be determining, it too must be concrete. It appears that the 'conjuncture' is something 'concrete' outside the structure, what then is it? How does structural determination limit this concrete class struggle and its effects?

Poulantzas not only has no answers to these questions, he simply does not recognise them as problems. Class determination is the general determination by the structure, but, if this general determination exhausted the possible concrete effects, then the effect of this position would be just like that of economistic Marxism. Class position is therefore introduced to qualify this possibility but it is not theorised. It is merely a means of hedging any bets made on the basis of class determination.

Poulantzas argues that class determination cannot be reduced to class position and, therefore, that the structure of 'instances' and its effects (classes, social division of labour) cannot be reduced to effects of concrete class practice and class struggle. However, we have seen that 'classes exist only in class struggle' and, Poulantzas goes on to say: 'From the start structural class determination involves, economic, political and ideological class struggle, and these struggles are all expressed in the form of class positions in the conjuncture' (p. 16). Poulantzas says explicitly that class determination involves the class struggle and that these struggles are 'expressed' in class positions in the conjuncture. 'Expression' here is ambiguous. *Either* it means that these struggles give rise to class positions, and, therefore, class determination determines class position. *Or*, it means that class struggles take the form of the positions of classes in conjunctures, in which case class positions determine (at least in part) class determination. Either way class determination 'involves' class struggle. But we have seen that class struggle can only be concrete, can only involve *class positions*. The structural determination of classes, if this concept is to have any meaning cannot be reduced to the class struggle.

What can it mean to say class determination 'involves' class struggle? Two positions are possible. Firstly, class determination forms and limits the class struggles – ultimately class struggles and the 'horizon' of class positions are effects of the structure. This has exactly the same effect as economism – social classes and political forces 'representing' social classes are ultimately equated. Class position merely gives 'room for manœuvre', that is, a let-out clause. Secondly, the class struggles form class determination to a greater or larger degree (this year's class determination is last year's class struggle). But class struggles must take the form of *class positions*. Hence class position forms class determination: class position and class determination are therefore involved in a relation of circularity, there can be no rigorous difference between them. This Poulantzas refuses as a voluntarist reduction of class determination to class position (cf. p. 201). Either, class position is a subsidiary difference from a basically determinant class determination, or class position and class determination are in essence one. In either case Poulantzas contradicts himself. Class determination/class position distinction is *ad hoc*: it is an attempt to avoid the effects of economism without the theoretical means of doing so. The result is utter incoherence.

There are two possible avenues of solution to this problem of the relation of class determination and class position suggested in *Classes in Contemporary Capitalism*: the first is Poulantzas's use of the concept of 'reproduction' and the second is the notion of 'concepts of strategy'. We will consider these in turn.

I. *Reproduction*

Central in the question of reproduction for Poulantzas is the reproduction of the relations of production. In this he follows Althusser's 'Ideology and Ideological State Apparatuses'.

The relations of production are the primary element in the structure of a mode of production and have the central place in the determination of social classes. The question of the reproduction of the relations of production is therefore central for the mode of existence of social classes. Poulantzas defines the role of the political and ideological instances, acting through the relations of production, in the determination of social classes as follows:

This dominant role of the relations of production over the productive forces and the labour process is what gives rise to the *constitutive* role of political and ideological relations in the structural determination of social classes (p. 21).

Thus political and ideological relations are *'constitutive'* (our emphasis) of the positions of classes in the social division of labour and therefore constitutive of class determination. The dominance of relations of production in modes of production and social division of labour is equivalent to the dominance of political and ideological relations. Poulantzas makes this clear:

The relations of production and the relationships which comprise them (economic ownership/possession) are expressed in the form of powers which derive from them, in other words class powers; these powers are *constitutively tied* to the political and ideological relations which sanction and legitimize them. These relations are not simply added on to relations of production that are 'already there', *but are themselves present*, in a form specific to each mode of production, *in the constitution of the relations of production* (p. 2).

Political and ideological relations are constitutive of the relations of production and the 'class powers' which these relations represent. Economic relations are 'constituted' (to what degree we are not told) by political and ideological relations: these relations must be conceived as forms of political/ideological domination.

Poulantzas conflates the relations of production with their political and ideological conditions of existence. Relations of production become relations of 'class powers' — political/ideological domination. Poulantzas is correct to argue that relations of production (possession and separation) do depend on legal forms (property) and political conditions (appropriation/defence of property). However, it is the definite economic *form* of these relations and the economic *consequences* of a definite form of possession (separation of workers from means of subsistence, wage labour, appropriation of profit) which constitute class relations between agents. Poulantzas reverses the classic economistic position in which the political/ideological conditions of existence of the economy are governed and given by the economic level itself (the other levels being subordinate 'superstructures'). Here instead the conditions of existence of the dominant element of the economic level, the relations of production, are given by political and ideological relations (these relations are *'constitutive'* of the production relations). Political and ideological forms create the *possibility* of relations of production, conceived as class 'powers', by creating 'sanctions and legitimations' for these powers. Political and ideological relations constitute the *form* of *domination*. 'Class powers' are conceived as a form of domination. Hence Poulantzas conceives of the factory as characterised by a 'despotism' exercised by capital over the working class. Domination distributes the agents into dominators, servants of domination and the dominated. This introduction of a politicised conception of the relations of production enables Poulantzas later to differentiate crucial sections of the 'new petty bourgeoisie' from the working class. It also allows him as we shall see to conceive the relation of working class and capitalist class as in essence antagonistic and explosive (dominators and dominated); whereas a conception based on the economic *form* of wage labour could not limit exploited wage workers to those sections of the militant industrial proletariat which might appear to make his characterisation of working class domination plausible.

Poulantzas's conflation of the relations of production with their political/ideological conditions of existence has an effect which is parallel to that of vulgar Marxist economism. Economism subordinates the political level to economic relations. Class positions are formed at the level of the economic structure and reflected in the political. The political is economised – the same class struggle can be read in both levels. Poulantzas conflates political and economic relations but instead introjects political forms as constitutive of the economic. Here again the possibility of a direct translation is created. The economic thus politicised provides the fundamental battle lines of the class struggle in the relation of dominators and dominated. This explains the fundamental class determination of the working class as the only class which is revolutionary to the end. While the relations of production are politicised they still occupy the *place of the economic*. Economic classes, through class determination – itself political/ideological – have political 'destinies' attached to them. Poulantzas as we shall see is not denying economism, but merely complicating it. His positions have exactly the same methods and effects as economistic class analysis. Except, that when it comes to the crunch he takes cover behind the political differences introduced by 'class position'.

The constitutive role of the political and the ideological in the formation of relations of production and the determination of social classes is an effect of the structure of the social totality. The global structure of the instances determines the economic. Politics and ideology are 'present in' the relations of production in 'the form specific to each mode of production'. This specific form is the action of the global structure of the mode. All modes have a specific necessary form of class determination which is a function of their structure. Poulantzas here retains Althusser's conception of the global structure of a mode of production determining the form and the place of the instances 'represented' in it. He retains, therefore, a basic concept associated with structural causality. With this difference. In Althusser it is the economic as global structure which is 'determinant in the last instance'. In Poulantzas it is the combination of the three instances, the totality, tripartite, which is determinant.

Poulantzas's concept of reproduction registers this conflation of the relations of production with their political and ideological conditions of existence. He derides conceptions of the analysis in vol. 2 of *Capital* as an economic process as 'superficial' (p. 27). The profundity of his own reading is, however, asserted not argued.

The central question in reproduction is the reproduction of the *relations* of production, the continuation of the social division of labour as a form of domination:

The process of production and exploitation is at the same time a process of the reproduction of the relations of political and ideological domination (p. 21).

Reproduction of the relations of production is conceived as the continuation of the political and ideological determinants of classes:

Reproduction, being understood as the extended reproduction of social classes, immediately means reproduction of the political and ideological relations of class determination (p. 27).

The concept of reproduction, reproducing the determinations of the structure, does not in fact enable Poulantzas to escape the class determination/class position dilemma – indeed, it sharpens it. Poulantzas makes the *class struggle* the fundamental arena and means of the reproduction of social classes:

We can say that there is a primary and fundamental reproduction of social classes in and by the class struggle, in which extended reproduction of the structure (including the production relations) operates, and which governs the functioning and role of the (state) apparatuses (p. 29).

The concrete forms of this reproduction depend on the particular evolution of definite class struggles:

To say that the primary reproduction of social classes depends on the class struggle also means that its concrete forms depend on the history of the social formation (p. 30).

Classes only exist in and can only be defined in the class struggle. The class struggle, 'the motor of history' (p. 27), reproduces the form of class relations. It does so by the successful maintenance of class powers – of positions of domination and subordination. This struggle must take place through *class positions*, it is the struggle of the actual class forces in a definite social formation. Class positions *must* have an effect on the form of social classes, on their reproduction, for otherwise they would be no more than epiphenomena and we would be back with an, at best complicated, economism. Therefore, the class struggle and the positions taken by classes in it must determine class determination. Yet the structure constitutes class determination and this assigns limits to the class positions. Yet the structure – in the concept of reproduction – is conceived as a domination of 'class powers', a domination which can only exist in class struggle. Class struggle and the class positions taken in it cannot be epiphenomenal and must have real effects on the future form of social classes. Poulantzas is caught in an unclosable circle, a circularity he needs to complete but dare not. The problem of the connection of class determination and class position is in essence the problem of the relation of practices to the structure and this remains theoretically unresolved.

II. 'CONCEPTS OF STRATEGY'

The articulation of the structural determination of classes and of class positions within the social formation, the locus of existence of conjunctures, requires particular concepts. I shall call these *concepts of strategy*, embracing in particular such phenomena as class polarisation and class alliance (p. 24).

These concepts are specific to *political* analysis and to definite social formations in definite conjunctures:

These concepts are not of the same status as those with which we have dealt up till now: whether a class . . . forms part of a power bloc, or part of the people, will depend on the social formation, its stages, phases and conjunctures (p. 24).

General concepts of class structure and determination appear to be modified in 'concrete' conditions. But, as we have seen, if class determination is to be a *determination* it must be as concrete as anything else.

In fact, the way Poulantzas conducts his investigations removes the place of 'concepts of strategy', for it, in effect, abolishes the specificity of the political situation on which these concepts are predicated. The class determination/class position distinction complicates and causes difficulties for Poulantzas's general theory of classes: it is incoherent and unstable. The concept of class position, however, merely qualifies (and threatens) an analysis which has exactly the same effects as classic economism. Poulantzas assigns classes and fractions political roles as a consequence of their social (economic) place. His political conclusion necessarily leaves analysis at the level of 'objective polarisation'. The relation of monopoly and non-monopoly capital at the economic level assigns these fractions their political roles, as dominant and subordinate fractions of capital. The 'objective polarisation', that is the effects of economic position and conditions, assigns fractions of the new petty bourgeoisie their possible political places.

Poulantzas's economism in effect assigns the strategic social locations of the 'power bloc' and 'the people' in advance. It can provide no 'concepts of strategy', concepts appropriate to definite political situations, since its sociologism assigns the possible politics and its limits to each social group (with the notion of class positions as a get-out clause and source of theoretical incoherence). This analysis cannot deal with concrete political forces, apparatuses, parties, ideologies, or with concrete issues, political and economic problems, or rather, it can, but only negatively, through critique. Thus Poulantzas counters the PCF's sociologism with his own; he does not counter the PCF's *programme* with his own. What he counters to the PCF's position is abstract revolutionism and the notion of a revolutionary class alliance led by the working *class*. The political form of this 'alliance' is left to the movement to settle. *Classes*, however, do not have programmes or hold congresses, they cannot 'lead' anything. Poulantzas simply reproduces the slogans of ultra-left Marxism.

Having considered at some length the problems of Poulantzas's conception of the relation of classes and politics these problems will be exemplified in his discussion of the petty bourgeoisie and the bourgeoisie. Poulantzas, as we have seen, gets into three related difficulties:

(i) he uses political and ideological criteria to reinforce sociologistic

distinctions of the political possibilities of social classes
conceived at the level of the economy;

(ii) he refuses the immediate consequences of this by his distinction
of class determination and class position, which being unstable
threatens his general position;

(iii) he proceeds in analysis to assign strategic places to classes on
the basis of their social position, using this to make political
criticisms of concrete political programmes, and then uses the
class determination/class position distinction to refuse to follow-
up rigorously the political consequences of his own
'economism'.

The 'New Petty Bourgeoisie'

The old and new petty bourgeoisies form one basic class grouping, not
because of a common position in economic relations, but because their
economic positions have basically similar political and ideological
effects. The petty bourgeoisie is neither part of the working class nor of
the capitalist class: its class determination situates it in an ambivalent
relationship to these two basic classes: '. . . the petty bourgeoisie has no
long-run autonomous class political position' (p. 297). It follows that:

. . . the class positions taken by the petty bourgeoisie must necessarily be
located in the balance of forces between the bourgeoisie and the working class,
and thus link up (by acting for or against) either with the class positions of the
bourgeoisie or with those of the working class (p. 297).

The petty bourgeoisie as a whole occupies an ambivalent position; the
determinants of which pole of the class struggle fractions of this class
will attach themselves to, are to be found in the objective social
differentiation this class is undergoing. This 'polarisation', essentially a
differentiation of economic conditions, establishes 'cleavages' in the
class, which predispose fractions to one or other of the main class
positions:

these cleavages thus fall along the boundaries of the fractions of the new
bourgeoisie, certain of which present objective preconditions for the adoption
of proletarian class positions (p. 303).

These 'objective preconditions' predispose the fractions in question in a certain political direction, but the political positions taken by these fractions may in the concrete case be different.

This analysis follows the classic line of economism: *differentiation at the level of the economic establishes the 'objective preconditions' for political differentiation*. The petty bourgeoisie is an ambivalent force. How the fractions of this class will place themselves politically depends on the concrete circumstances, on the balance of forces between the two main classes. But what determines the positions of these two main classes? As in classic economism, it is the fundamental situation of the class at the economic level. Poulantzas says:

Even under the effects of bourgeois ideology, there still always breaks through in the working class what Lenin referred to as 'class instinct'. This is simply the constant resurgence, in its practices, of the class determination of that class which suffers, in the factory and in material production, the extraction of surplus value (p. 238).

Class determination creates class *'experience'* or *'instinct'* which imposes (in the long run) the limits of 'class interests' on the class positions of the working class. That is why the working class is 'the only class which is revolutionary to the end'. This notion of class 'experience' depends on the immediacy of social relations to the subjects involved in them (we have criticised this notion extensively elsewhere and will not dwell on it here). The working class experiences in the 'despotism' (p. 229) of the factory the fundamental conditions of the class struggle. Poulantzas says, for example: 'The work of management and supervision under capitalism is the direct reproduction, within the process of production itself, of the political relations between the capitalist class and the working class' (pp. 227–8). We noted above the effect of this politicisation of economic relations, its parallel with economism. *Poulantzas's politicisation of basic economic relations allows him to locate the essence of the class struggle, its perpetual source, at the level of the immediate capital/labour relation. As a consequence classes as categories of agents at the level of the relations of production are ultimately equated with political forces and are given necessary long run political positions.* The class 'interests' and the long run political positions of both the bourgeoisie and the proletariat can be read-off from their places in capitalist production relations.

'The Bourgeoisies and the State'

Poulantzas's discussion of the fractions of the bourgeoisie further exemplifies this derivation of political differentiation from economic differentiation. Poulantzas's analysis of the relation of fractions of the capitalist class to one another and to the state is conducted as a critique of the PCF's position. For Poulantzas the economic analysis that underlies the notion of an anti-monopoly alliance is incorrect. For the PCF the dominance of the monopolies and their fusion with the state apparatus creates the conditions for a broad anti-monopoly alliance, incorporating small business and non-monopoly capital. This 'alliance' is a form of economistic populism; its elements are supposed to be united by a common economic domination by the monopolies and by the effective exclusion from state power which is a function of big capital's annexation of the state. The battle lines are thus the 'people' versus the monopolies, an alliance of classes in a struggle for an 'advanced democracy'.

Poulantzas counters this with a leftist economism. It is criticised as incorrect because it gets the relation of monopoly and non-monopoly capital wrong. The balance of class forces is derived by Poulantzas from changes and trends in the economic structure (which are far from rigorously analysed). The forms of concentration and centralisation of non-monopoly capital, give the balance of the class fractions of the bourgeoisie. Economic dominance gives the basic form of political hegemony. At the same time as he derives the balance of forces from the forms of concentration and centralisation, Poulantzas explains both the results of and the limits to this process in terms of a political policy of monopoly capital: monopoly capital is forced to support and sustain non-monopoly forms as a result of the dominant contradiction with the working class (cf. p. 149). Economic fractions are thus converted directly into political agents. Poulantzas says:

The forms and tempo of the concentration process, as expressed in the forms of persistence of non-monopoly capital, are often simply strategic measures that serve the political interests of monopoly capital, by ensuring its political hegemony over the bourgeoisie as a whole and maintaining the political cohesion of the power bloc in the face of the working class (p. 146).

Monopoly capital is unified as a Machiavellian economic/political force capable of calculation and *policy*. However, 'monopoly capital' *means* the dominant enterprises in certain key branches of production. These enterprises do not choose the conditions of competition or its results. They can no more decide to 'preserve' non-monopoly capital than they can decide to preserve themselves. Trade organisations and state bodies may attempt to preserve specific enterprises which are uncompetitive on the prevailing social scale; they may or may not succeed in keeping them going. That is another matter entirely. Poulantzas has made the source of this process (often a response to *trade union* pressure) a fraction of capital with a definite *political* policy. Does this economic-political force exist? He makes no attempt to demonstrate that there is *at the political level* a unified force – 'monopoly capital'.

It is not accidental that Poulantzas uses the concept of 'hegemony' to explain the dominance of monopoly capital. He argues against the PCF that the state is relatively autonomous from the monopolies, that it is not simply their creature (p. 164). At the same time monopoly capital exercises 'hegemony' over the ruling power bloc. The great advantage of this concept is that one can postulate a relationship of domination without explaining what its concrete mechanisms are. 'Hegemony' is exercised by class fraction over fraction, relatively independent of state apparatuses. The effect of this hegemony or domination, a power exercised independently of the state machine, is to restrict the freedom and policies of that machine *vis-à-vis* the dominant class fraction (p. 168). The state in consequence is less able to play the role of an apparatus of class hegemony in general. Its capacity to 'represent' the various fractions of the dominant power bloc is thus reduced. Increasingly subordinate to the interests of the monopolies it is less able to meet the needs of the other capitalist fractions or the masses. One may ask what differentiates this from the PCF's state monopoly capitalism? The answer is the hegemonisation of non-monopoly capital through its economic dependence and on the basis of its common class interest in opposing the working class. Poulantzas's difference from the PCF in essence concerns the nature of the essential class 'interests' of capitalists in general, whether monopolists or not.

B. EXPLOITATION AND PRODUCTIVE LABOUR

Poulantzas defines the working class as that class which performs productive labour in the mode of production, productive labour is labour 'which gives rise to the specific and dominant form of exploitation' (p. 20). Thus far, Poulantzas's position tallies with that of Marx: productive labour in capitalism is that labour which produces surplus value. Poulantzas draws the obvious conclusion from the theory of productive and unproductive labour:

It follows that it is not wages that define the working class economically: wages are a form of distribution of the social product, corresponding to market relations and the forms of 'contract' governing the purchase and sale of labour power. Although every worker is a wage labourer, every wage earner is certainly not a worker, for not every wage earner is engaged in productive labour (p. 20).

The productive/unproductive labour distinction enables us in the first instance to separate the working class from other wage earners and employees. Poulantzas follows Marx in excluding commercial employees and providers of services from productive labour. Commercial workers do not produce commodities but merely circulate them. They cannot add to value and in consequence they are paid out of the *faux frais* of capitalist circulation. Service employees are not productive because they do not produce surplus value but exchange services for revenue. State employees are likened to service workers.

For Marx productive labour is labour which produces surplus value and therefore which takes the form of commodities. The production of commodities and employment by a capitalist are Marx's criteria of productive labour. Marx says:

It follows from what has been said that the designation of labour as *productive labour* has absolutely nothing to do with the *determinate content* of the labour . . . *The same* kind of labour may be *productive* or *unproductive* . . . A singer who sells her song for her own account is an *unproductive labourer*. But the same singer commissioned by an entrepreneur to sing in order to make money for him is a *productive labourer*; for she produces capital (*Theories of Surplus Value*, Vol. I, p. 401).

Marx gives examples of the 'literary proletarian' and the hack denizen of a 'teaching factory' as other illustrations of this point. Evidently having teachers at the Berlitz, actors, singers, hack writers, chefs, etc., as part of the working class, under the 'dominant capitalist relation of exploitation', does not appeal to Poulantzas. The working class defined by the criterion of 'productive labour' would not correspond to that social grouping Poulantzas wishes to differentiate from other employees – the industrial proletariat.

In consequence Poulantzas 'adds' a criterion to Marx's definition of productive labour (claiming that it has been present, in effect, in Marx's *Capital* all along):

We shall say that productive labour, in the capitalist mode of production is labour that produces surplus-value while *directly reproducing the material elements that serve as the substratum of the relation of exploitation: labour that is directly involved in material wealth* (p. 216).

Poulantzas's new criterion amounts to saying that commodities which produce surplus value will be limited to reproducible material products of labour.

Poulantzas attempts to argue for his exclusions following the example of works of art:

. . . it is still the case that, with the generalisation of the commodity form under capitalism, labour may take the commodity form without producing surplus-value for capital. This is particularly the case with the work of painters, artists and writers, which is concretised in a work of art or a book, i.e. in a commodity form, even though what is involved here are services exchanged against revenue . . . In other words, although all capitalist productive labour takes the commodity form, this does not mean that all commodities represent productive labour (p. 219).

But these remarks say nothing about the 'teaching factory', the hack publishing house, the theatrical enterprise, the commercial hospital. These enterprises sell *commodities* to make profits – lectures, books, dramatic performances, surgical operations, etc. – not services exchanged against revenue. If it is argued that the purchase of these commodities merely circulates the portion of surplus value consumed by the capitalist class (proletarians never read, or get ill), the same could be said of all 'luxury' consumption. The workers at the car division of Rolls-Royce are providing 'services against revenue'? Further, the example of works of art is irrelevant. The examples we have cited are all arguably *material and reproducible*: otherwise *The Mousetrap* would have closed after the first night and we could read about *the* appendectomy, but not have one. A Raphael or Michelangelo is unique: it has a fetish value and a price determined by competition to acquire the object in question. A Boots' painting is a commodity like any other. These counter examples cannot be written-off as 'services exchanged against revenue' or as unique non-reproducible creations. Poulantzas fails to recognise that Marx's concept of *use-value* is problematic. If it does not mean socially useful (which implies some evaluative standard) then it must mean saleable. Any commodity which sells must by definition have a use-value and therefore some definite and reproducible existence-form (even if it be sequences of sounds – or, if capitalists ever colonised psychoanalysis, silence). A lecture or a massage represent use-values to their consumers. They are, furthermore, reproducible commodities.

Evidently Poulantzas wants to exclude masseusses, private college lecturers, etc., from his 'working class'. In the United States health care and education remain less penetrated by state agencies and non-commodity forms than they are, say, in this country. In addition the capitalisation of entertainment, sports and vacationing is highly developed. Nurses, teachers, professional sports players, hotel workers, etc., are employees of enterprises which sell commodities in order to produce profits. These commodities are consumed by wage earners just like bread or toothpaste. They cannot, any more than bread or toothpaste, be conceived as 'services exchanged against revenue'. Elements of Poulantzas 'new petty bourgeoisie' could therefore be considered, on the criterion of productive labour (and irrespective of its merits), part of the working class.

Productive Labour and Class Determination – Engineers and Technicians

The case of engineers and technicians is even more interesting – it illustrates all too clearly what work Poulantzas's 'criteria' of class definition are actually doing. Having restricted the content of Marx's concept of productive labour Poulantzas finds it still includes inpermissible elements in the working class. Productive labour therefore cannot rigorously define working class membership. To draw the 'boundaries separating this class [the new petty bourgeoisie] from the working class' (p. 224) other than 'economic' criteria are needed:

Economic relations such as the distinction between productive and unproductive labour are not sufficient to delimit the class boundaries between the working class and certain fringe sections of the new petty bourgeoisie, i.e. those fringes that are themselves directly involved in the process of material production. This is the case with supervisory staff and with engineers and technicians (p. 224).

Although these agents perform productive labour, their structural class determination, their place in the social division of labour, separates them from the working class:

the reason why these agents do not belong to the working class is that their structural class determination and the place they occupy in the social division of labour are marked by the dominance of the political relations that they maintain over the aspect of productive labour in the division of labour (p. 228).

These personnel serve as auxiliaries of bourgeois class power, and their role is conceived as that of agents of bourgeois *political* domination at the level of the factory:

The despotism of the factory is the form taken by political relations in the extended production of social classes, actually on the site where the relations of production and exploitation are constructed (p. 229).

Poulantzas *politicises* the work of co-ordination and supervision. The foreman is an agent of bourgeois class power at the level of the factory and the policeman at the level of the state. Engineers and technicians even if they do not directly control the workers are part of a process separating them from their conditions of work and subordinating them to an ideological class 'knowledge'. For Poulantzas the distinction between mental and manual labour has nothing to do with any attributes of the tasks involved; it means simply the ideological/political subordination of the working class to a hierarchy created by the bourgeoisie. This distinction is not a division of *labour*, it has no technical necessity but is a form of existence of class domination. It is a necessary product of and form of bourgeois social relations – the way in which the capitalist social division of labour manifests itself. The working class is the class *outside* this hierarchy of supervision and co-ordination, it is the force which this collection of apparatuses acts upon to subordinate.

We may note in passing that if this division is a necessary form of the *capitalist* social division of labour, the position of all the 'socialist' countries becomes most questionable. All socialist states, including China, exhibit this separation of the work of planning and execution. Forms of centralisation of decision-making in politics and the economy, forms of exclusion of the masses of the people, whether it be 'palace politics' in Peking or the power of the managers of enterprises in the USSR, exist in socialist countries. Poulantzas does not rigorously face this question. Clearly, it raises the conditions of existence of the distinction between mental and manual labour as a problem. If this distinction is necessarily a product of a *capitalist* social division of labour what are we to make of the construction of *socialist* relations of production by means of it? One can, either, follow Bettelheim and write off the Soviet Union (and China, romanticism apart) as a state 'capitalist' society dominated by the 'state bourgeoisie', or one cannot make this division solely a function of capitalist social relations.

The general consequences of Poulantzas's *politicisation* of *supervision* will be discussed in the next section. Here we may merely note again that political/ideological relations are introduced to differentiate economic classes at the level of the economic. In this crucial case (Poulantzas calls it a question of 'fringe sections', but every 'fringe' is vital not secondary since it reveals the criteria of differentiation) 'class determination' comes to mean not position in the relations of production (which must be discounted since it does not allow us to differentiate) but 'function' in the enterprise. Poulantzas develops and deploys his criteria so as to restrict the concept of 'working class' to a definite pre-existent social category, the industrial manual workers.

C. POULANTZAS AND THE 'POLITICAL'

Poulantzas's use of political/ideological relations to differentiate and constitute social classes reveals the plasticity of his concept of the 'political'. He derides institutional analysis. Yet his foremen and engineers derive their positions from an institutional hierarchy. He can identify their specialist *function* only by their organisational position. Where workers *supervise themselves* (through certain forms of methods of payment and/or gang-labour systems) to a greater or larger extent, this necessary function is not institutionally visible. Having so identified them, Poulantzas refuses to accept the specificity of their positions and powers in definite capitalist enterprises. They become servants of the global domination of capital. The 'despotism' of the factory is but a manifestation of the despotism of capital. The foreman represents class hegemony in miniature. The specificity of the functions of co-ordination and their localisation in definite enterprises vanish into a global domination of the capitalist class. In consequence the significance for the socialist movement of a whole series of struggles is denied. Methods of organising and surpervising production cannot be reformed and transformed by the actions of the workers: self-supervision and group payment, 'workers control', workers co-operatives trading in capitalist markets are all evidently reformist and pointless, rather than being advanced sectors of trade-union struggle. In facing the foreman the worker confronts bourgeois power itself. This hyper-politicises struggle at the level of the economic.

Class domination is conceived by Poulantzas in terms of class 'power': this 'power' is without localisation, the different 'apparatuses' (p. 25), churches, trade unions, publishing houses, are merely forms of its manifestation. These apparatuses '. . . do not possess a "power" of their own, but materialise and concentrate class relations, relations which are precisely what is embraced by the concept "power". The state is not an "entity" with an intrinsic instrumental essence, but is itself a relation, more precisely the condensation of a class relation' (p. 26).

The state is a 'condensation' of a relation between classes, a relation of domination. Politics is placed beyond the 'political' into a global relation of *social classes*. This has two effects:

(i) state apparatuses are discounted *vis-à-vis* the global relation of domination of the classes, they merely *condense* this domination in an institutional form;

(ii) state power and class power are equated, hence any apparatus serving class domination can be considered as a *state* apparatus, the family or the media, for example (in this Poulantzas follows the line of Althusser's *ISAs* paper).

It follows that a class 'power' without form or localisation can be invested in any concrete institution or 'apparatus' without changing its form. This 'apparatus' then performs its social role in the maintenance of class 'hegemony'. Class 'power' or 'hegemony' has no definite conditions of existence. It emerges from social relations as a whole, from the hegemonic class itself. Politics is conceived as the global domination of one *class* by another much in the way that one *subject* can be conceived as dominated by another (as in Hegel or Weber). Such domination is a *relationship* (a form of intersubjectivity) – it has no conditions of existence other than itself. This global domination of *classes* reveals the discounting of the political itself. As we saw at the beginning of this paper, one never encounters classes as forces active in politics. The political (in the sense of the state and political apparatuses) survives for Poulantzas as one form of manifestation of the class struggle among others. Indeed, for all Poulantzas's talk of the 'relative automony of the political', his current position amounts to just as rigorous a sociologisation of politics as classic economistic Marxism.

The effect of the discounting of state institutions and political organisations, the globalising of the 'political' into all forms of social relations and the generalising of *state* apparatuses beyond the constitutional confines of the state (*ISAs*), is to erase the possibility of the classic Marxist forms of political calculation we find in Lenin and Mao Tse-tung. Poulantzas's conception of the 'political' and of 'class power' creates the problem that the political 'instance' is everywhere and nowhere. The specificity of state apparatuses is discounted. The '*state*' cannot be defined at the level of institutions or apparatuses (they are merely forms of manifestation of class power) but can be defined only by its *function*. The 'state' is assigned the function of cohesion:

The principal role of the state apparatuses is to maintain the unity and cohesion of the social formation by concentrating and sanctioning class domination, and in this way reproducing social relations, i.e. class relations (p. 25).

This statement overturns Poulantzas's expressed theoretical-political allegiances for it would have pleased Hilferding and made Lenin weep. First and foremost the *state exists*, it is a definite apparatus to be confronted, and not a function. State power and state institutions are not coincidental; there can be 'powerless' institutions. State institutions nevertheless represent the means of action of state power just as political parties, organisations and groups define the forces that are active in any given political situation. Although the state/civil society distinction is created by state legislation, instituting a 'private' sphere, the legal/constitutional/organisational form of the state does have real effects. In general it defines the apparatuses of the state and their limits.

To ignore the specific *form* of the state is to neglect two vital facts: that state power has conditions of existence and limits. State power has *conditions of existence*: it depends upon definite forms of organisation and means of coercion to be a *power*. State power also has *limits*: its dependence on such *definite* apparatuses limits both the forms of exercise of power (power is limited to the means available) and those who can exercise it. State power cannot be appropriated without struggle (whatever the character of the forces attempting to seize it) and it is separated in definite ways from the members of 'civil society', who cannot substitute themselves for it or appropriate it at will. The notion of 'class power' is subject, neither to the limit of conditions of existence (since it exists beyond all apparatuses), nor to the limit of access (since only the class *as a class*, never definite bodies of its members, is conceived as an agent). I would assert that, on the contrary, outside specific institutional forms state power does not exist: institutions represent the means of its existence and exercise. Further, I would assert that whilst functionaries, organisations and individuals may have access to this power (for example, wealthy capitalists may 'influence' decisions or trade unionists may force a certain policy upon an apparatus) *classes* never do. Classes do not have 'interests' and are not political actors. Only definite organisations, or even individual agents, are political forces – and we have seen the problems entailed in the notion of 'representation'.

To *take state power* Lenin insisted is always to subordinate by force or to neutralise through political means definite agencies of coercion and means of control. It is to subordinate army, police, courts, communications, etc., by means of other apparatuses with definite powers of coercion and organisation (thus the Russian railway workers in 1917 frustrated Kornilov without directly defeating him by force of arms). Any organiser of a coup d'état (whether it be revolutionary or not) has no illusions about the specificity of state power to definite institutions. Poulantzas repeats the slogans about 'smashing' the state but he conjures away the specificity of *what it is* that is to be smashed. Far from asserting the specificity of the political the ultimate effect of his position is to deny it.

WOMEN IN THE LABOUR PROCESS AND CLASS STRUCTURE

Jean Gardiner

What distinguishes the Marxist from the sociological concept of class is its location within a political theory of movement and change. The usefulness of any particular definition of class must be judged in terms of the degree to which it enables us to understand and intervene within the forces for change in our society. Conversely it is our involvement in the movements within the society which enable us to sharpen and develop our analysis of class. The movement of women, of which the women's liberation movement is the most cohesive expression, is one of the distinctive political features of industrial capitalist societies such as Britain in the 1970s. This paper is an attempt to apply to our analysis of class and the labour process some of the insights we have gained from that movement.

We see classes as aggregates of people distinguished from each other by the place they occupy in a system of social production, i.e. by their relationship to the labour process, to the means of production and to the wealth and resources that are produced in the labour process. However, as it stands, this definition does not give us criteria for judging the key distinctive qualities that separate one class from another. Thus, on the one hand, it has been compatible with a definition of the working class as productive workers. For example Poulantzas defines the working class exclusively as those workers producing surplus value who are limited, according to him, to those directly involved in material production. Other Marxists have defined the working class as the sellers of labour power. According to this definition the fundamental class division in capitalist society is between those who own and control the means of production and those who, owning nothing but their own labour power, are forced to sell it to the capitalist class in exchange for wages.

I would argue that much of the confusion surrounding the concept of class stems from the impossibility of defining in a one dimensional way the place individuals occupy in a system of social production. Thus however narrowly one defined the working class one would still find within that aggregate divisions and subdivisions of both a material and ideological kind. In the circumstances two responses are possible. Either one abandons the concept of class altogether in the face of the complexity of concrete experience, which would imply abandoning a class analysis of society, or one adopts a broad definition of class with a commitment to examine and give political weight to the divisions and subdivisions within class. In adopting the latter approach I am accepting a definition of the working class as those people dependent on the sale of labour power for survival.

What follows is divided into three sections. First I want to look at the distinct relationship of women and men to the sale of labour power. Then I will look briefly at the sexual division within the labour process. The final section will suggest some of the political implications of changes in the class structure and labour process.

Throughout I want to emphasise the relationship between the family and the class structure since this is central to understanding the specific position of women and men. The reproduction of the class structure of capitalism is dependent on the family unit in at least three ways. First the family is the economic unit for the reproduction of classes from generation to generation. Women bearing and rearing children and their children are economically supported via the family unit, usually by the male breadwinner. Secondly the family reproduces the class structure socially and culturally both because the family is one of the major areas for socialisation of children and because marriage takes place largely within class. Thirdly the family plays a key role which has distinct implications for men and for women in the daily maintenance of the working class through both redistribution of wages and domestic labour.

THE WAGE LABOUR RELATION

Within a capitalist society the wage labour relation between individual workers and employers is the dominant social relationship in the sphere of production because of the pattern of ownership and economic control. The development of capitalism has required a growing mass of people able and willing to become wage labourers. Both the family and the state have evolved as institutions to facilitate this process, both on a day to day and on a generational basis. Here I shall concentrate on the role of the family.

In the first place the average wage payable in capitalist production, even for men, has consistently been lower than would be necessary for adequate subsistence if men had not also been able to rely on the unpaid domestic services of women. Even in recent years with capitalist production relations spreading to more and more service areas, for instance, catering, cleaning, laundry, ways have not been found to cheapen the cost of production adequately to convert these labour processes entirely into commodity production.

Also whilst capitalism has required a growing pool of wage labourers it is unable to offer secure employment prospects to all the women and men in this pool and persistently recreates a reserve of unemployed. The family has facilitated the recreation of this reserve, not just amongst women, as has often been noted, but also amongst men. The fact that families increasingly depend on women's wages as well as men's makes it easier for them to survive when men are out of work. This may have been a major factor explaining the ease with which mass male unemployment has been accepted since the late sixties.

The redistributional role of the family within the working class is even more crucial for reproduction of that class on a generational basis. Within the family wages are redistributed from the individual worker (usually male) to children and childrearer (usually female). Women within the family provide the bulk of the care and early education of young children in the absence of an adequate provision of nurseries and nursery schools. They continue to have responsibility for the extra-school care of older children too.

A number of points of relevance to our analysis of the class structure and women's place within it emerge from all this. Even if we abstract from other non-capitalistic production relations coexisting in a capitalist society, such as self-employed workers, family workers, we find that the relationship of the mass of people to the system of social production is considerably more complex than the wage labour relation as normally described. The working class as I have defined it will consist at any one time of both those who are selling their labour power and those not directly involved in but dependent upon that sale, in other words women houseworkers, children, unemployed, the sick, the old. Whilst they are of the working class, in the sense I have defined it, these groups have a vicarious relationship to the sale of labour power which must affect their position both materially and ideologically.

Let us look at the implications of this for women. One of the most striking features of the class structure in the last thirty years has been the growth of wage work amongst women. Moreover all the growth has occurred amongst married women both because reserves of single women had already been tapped and because the rate of marriage itself was increasing. Thus a dual and somewhat contradictory process has been at work in which on the one hand more and more women have come to depend directly on the sale of their own labour power for all but a small portion of their adult lives whilst, on the other hand, dependence on marriage and commitment to domestic responsibilities has also spread to increasing numbers of women.

This contradictory process is reflected in the composition of the female wage labour force which I will discuss further below. One relevant feature to note here is that all the growth in female employment between 1960 and the mid seventies occurred amongst part-time workers (working for thirty hours a week or less) who are predominantly women with major domestic responsibilities *vis-à-vis* husbands and children. Moreover average earnings of full-time women workers relative to those of men have only risen very slightly in the last thirty years. Women earn only about two-thirds as much as men. Thus women workers' economic dependence on marriage has been maintained. The state has continued to reinforce this dependence through its taxation and social security provisions. The poor provision of socialised childcare has had the same effect, tying women to domestic labour.

I would argue that the approach of Marxists to analysis of class has tacitly acknowledged the dependent relationship of women to men without addressing any of the problems this relationship poses either theoretically or politically. For example women's class position has generally been equated with that of their husbands and the family implicitly taken as the unit for analysis of the class structure. But the distinct relationship of women and men to wage labour and the potential this raises for divergent interests within the family have not been dealt with. Nor has the significance of the increase in women's direct involvement in wage labour been addressed.

A new approach to the analysis of class is therefore crucial. We should recognise that women on account of their position in our society as houseworkers, childbearers, childrearers and dependents of men have a dual relationship to the class structure. On the one hand there is the direct involvement in wage labour which most women now experience throughout the bulk of their adult lives and on the other there is that aspect of their relationship to class which is mediated by the family, dependence on men and domestic labour. Because of this dual relationship women's consciousness of class will be distinct from men's and their involvement in class struggle will take different forms, for instance, campaigning for childcare facilities may assume an importance for women over and above fighting for wages and women may more readily than men be won for the fight against social service cuts. Moreover conflicts of interest arising within the family as a result of women's subordinate position within it have repercussions on the class struggle itself, for example, when women are prevented from full participation in the trade union movement by men's insistence that they stay at home to carry out their duties as wives. Thus any analysis of class which does not take account of divisions within the family fails to address important political issues. I will return to these in the last section of the paper.

THE SEXUAL DIVISION OF LABOUR

With the growth of women's employment the sexual division of labour, a division of labour originally located and still maintained within the family, has been extended to the social labour process. First let us be clear what is meant by sexual division of labour in this context.

Labour is distributed both horizontally between separate industries or labour processes and vertically within each labour process. Within both the horizontal and vertical distributions of labour, women and men are not evenly spread throughout but are unevenly concentrated in such a way that a large proportion of jobs are predominantly male or female. This uneven concentration is what we mean by the sexual division of labour. I would argue that it plays a major role in underpinning women's subordination to men in the society as a whole, in perpetuating divisions within the working class and in maintaining the political subordination of the working class as a whole.

The sexual division of labour as it has evolved within and between labour processes cannot be understood except in the context of the dual tendency described in the previous section, in other words, women coming increasingly to depend on the sale of their own labour power for a larger and larger part of their lives whilst dependence on marriage and commitment to domestic labour have also been extended. Thus women have been drawn into those jobs where pay is low as a result of a poor bargaining position (traditionally service employment in the state sector or industries where employment is in isolated small scale units, e.g. in offices and shops). This is an example of the way in which divisions within the working class are maintained since it is always the weakest groups who are drawn into jobs which provide the least potential for organisation. Thus the relative weakness and strength of different sections are perpetuated. To overcome these divisions requires the development of a political commitment within the trade union movement to the extension of trade unionism throughout the workforce.

One important aspect of the sexual division of labour is the implications it has for the distinct relationship of women and men to the development of society's productive forces. There are very few women employed in industries concerned with the application of science and technology to labour processes. Women are mostly engaged in producing consumer goods or services and not in the investment goods sector of the economy. In this way the sexual division of labour must limit the confidence women have in taking an active role in shaping the society they live in.

The sexual division of labour exists wherever women and men work together. Invariably it is men who occupy positions of authority and responsibility. It is probably most sharply defined in certain service occupations – sales work, administrative, clerical and professional jobs – which are organised along highly hierarchical lines. In these areas men have been predominant in positions entailing decision-making and authority whilst women have been mainly found carrying out routine operations often of a highly manual character (even when officially described as non-manual), for instance, typing and office machine operation. When the sexual division of labour takes this form, however limited male workers control over the labour process as a whole may be, they are placed in a position of considerable control over the women who work under them and are therefore less likely to challenge the hierarchical structure as a whole. For the women it is difficult to challenge the hierarchy without challenging male dominance which for most will be perceived as natural and inevitable.

In analysing the sexual division of labour we have to tackle two separate but related questions. First why do labour processes evolve to produce a given pattern of jobs? Secondly why are people drawn into specific jobs on the basis of their sex? The relationship between these two processes is quite complex because of the interaction between demand for labour and its supply.

On the one hand it is implicit in our analysis of class divisions that the employers of labour are both economically and politically dominant through their control and ownership of the means of production and their control of the state. Thus they are able to have a determining role in the evolution of labour processes and job structures. Yet they also have to take account of factors like the composition and degree of organisation of the workforce available to them. Thus the consciousness and actions of people in their jobs will influence the way those jobs evolve. For example, the job of secretary has become established over the years as a female job which incorporates many personal service elements reminiscent of women's traditional role in the family. If the labour available for this expanding area of work had been male instead of female it is unlikely that the job would have evolved in this way.

In examining the changing composition of the working class over the last twenty-five years we therefore have to ask what are the implications both of the transformation of the occupational structure and of the fact that nearly all the expansion in employment has occurred amongst women. What is the significance of the fact that the single largest occupational group at the beginning of the 1950s was engineering, a predominantly male job, whilst it is now clerical work, a mainly female job? What are the implications of parallel developments in the trade union movement with growth in organisation concentrated both amongst the so-called white-collar groups and also amongst women?

SOME POLITICAL IMPLICATIONS

I have tried to show how, in order to understand women's changing position in the labour process and class structure, we have to examine two aspects. The first is women's relationship to class as mediated by the family and dependence on men. The second is their direct involvement in the social labour process. I have argued that whilst their direct involvement in wage labour has increased, the significance of their distinct position in the family has in no way diminished. Indeed the wage-work women have been drawn into and the terms on which they have been employed have been to a large extent shaped by ideological and material forces that propel them in directions consistent with the sexual division of labour within the family. Thus women have, in the main, been drawn into work which is lacking in formal skills, low paid, often includes personal service elements, is frequently part-time, and in general lacks responsibility and authority.

However, there is one section of women for whom the pattern has been somewhat different. These are women who have been drawn into the greatly expanded further and higher education system, encouraged through that process to expect equal job opportunity with men and able subsequently, although still subject to sexual discrimination, to get sufficiently highly paid employment to remain economically independent of marriage. For this section of women, dependent on the sale of their labour power but not on marriage, the material basis for equality with working class men has begun to exist. This has enabled this section of women to take a leading role in challenging the sexism of the society. It is not surprising therefore that it is mainly amongst these women that direct involvement in the women's liberation movement has occurred. Within the working class as I have defined it these women are in a distinct economic position from the majority of women workers because of their independence from marriage. This does not, however, prevent common interests from being established on such issues as abortion and contraception, childcare, and discrimination at work.

Whilst the material conditions for equality with working-class men have continued to elude the majority of women workers, a new consciousness of both sexual and class oppression has begun to develop as a result of some of the changes I have described, and others outside the scope of this paper such as developments in contraception and abortion. A major aspect of this is the way in which women's relationship to the organised class struggle has become more direct and less mediated by men. The clearest manifestations of this development have been in the field of struggles over equal pay, equal job opportunity, union recognition, redundancy and cuts in public sector spending and employment. The developing consciousness of women involved in these struggles has been influenced both by the material change which have directly affected them and by the ideological and campaigning impact of the women's liberation movement, for instance through the Working Women's Charter campaign.

What I have tried to suggest is that it is impossible to understand women's class position without examining the ways in which sexual divisions shape women's concrete experience of class. It is thus inevitable both that women's consciousness of class will be informed by their oppression as a sex and that their involvement in class struggle, if it is to advance their position, must raise the question of how women's liberation is to be achieved. No socialist committed to the class struggle can afford to ignore this question.

I should like to thank the following people for helpful comments: Sarah Benton, Beatrix Campbell, Ronald Frankenberg, Jill Lewis, Barbara Taylor, Kate Young.

FURTHER READING

Communist Party, *Class Structure: Selected Articles from Marxism Today*, CP Pamphlet.

Conference of Socialist Economists, *On the Political Economy of Women*, CSE Pamphlet No. 2.

Coulson, Magas and Wainwright, 'Women and the Class Struggle', *New Left Review*, 89, pp. 59–72 (1975).

Department of Employment, *Women and Work: a Statistical Survey*, Manpower Paper 9, HMSO.

Gardiner, Jean, 'Women's Domestic Labour', *New Left Review*, 89, pp. 47–58 (1975).

Gardiner, Jean, *Reform or Revolution? Women in Society*, Course Unit, Open University, 1976.

Hunt, Judith, 'Women and Liberation', *Marxism Today* (November 1975).

Poulantzas, Nicos, *Classes in Contemporary Capitalism*, New Left Books, (London, 1975).

Seacombe, Wally, 'Housework under Capitalism', *New Left Review*, 83, pp. 3–24 (1974).

CLASS, INEQUALITY AND 'CORPORATISM'

John Westergaard

I

I shall begin by setting out two connected propositions. They form both the premises and the conclusions for this paper – though you may find yourselves thinking that, in trying to illustrate them, I take a rather roundabout route between start and finish.

First, as I see it, class is in essence a matter of inequality, inequality the very stuff of class. Different modes of production involve different modes of inequality: that hardly needs saying. But to refer to people's class situations within a particular mode of production has to be, I submit, to refer in the first instance to their locations in the structure of inequality characteristic of that mode of production. It must involve reference, before all else, to their places in a web of inequality, anchored in the prevailing relations of production, and made up of inequality of power, authority and influence, inequality of material conditions and security, inequality of opportunity and of access to cultural as well as material resources, contrasts between relative autonomy and relative dependence in life. Inequality is the hub of class because, above all, it is such disparities of position in a structure of inequality which generate endemic conflicts of class interest: conflicts that are inherent and perennially present whether, at particular points of the structure, at particular times and in particular circumstances, they are overt or latent; in active eruption, subdued, repressed or diverted; expressed in head-on confrontation or contained in a frame of institutionalised compromise.

My use of the phrases 'in the first instance', 'before all else', 'above all', is deliberate. I concede a need for some qualification. Class situations in a given mode of production may not be exhaustively described by reference only to location in the characteristic structure of inequality. It is possible, in the first place, for two or more categories of people to occupy broadly similar, perhaps even virtually identical, places in the structure of inequality; yet, because they play different parts in the chain of economic processes, to have interests inherently and logically at odds. The stances and policies for or against change in the current order in closest correspondence with their economic roles, by the criterion of long-run benefit to them, might diverge. That is conceivable. Routine white collar workers in commercial and in state employment in contemporary capitalist economies might, for example, constitute two such categories; their class situations would then be distinct, despite all similarities of condition with respect to inequality. But if the point is to have significance, it needs demonstration. It is not enough merely to point to a difference in economic roles, and on that basis in itself – by appeal only to definitional fiat – to postulate a difference in class situations. The relevance of the difference in economic roles to inherent interests has to be shown. There is the rub. For that in turn means to show that any clash of inherent interests deducible from this difference has the potential capacity to override, or substantially to diminish, the community of inherent interests arising from a common exposure to common conditions of life. At most, even so, the description of class situation by reference to economic role then augments, and in the process qualifies, the description by reference to location in the structure of inequality. It does not supplant it.

I do not want to take up time here by pursuing the converse case – where an identity or near-identity of economic roles may go with marked disparities of position in the structure of inequality. But were I to pursue it, my conclusion would be the same: the acid test will be that of relevance to inherent interests, from the consideration of which location in the prevailing web of inequality can neither be dismissed nor relegated to the periphery of analysis. I will, however, bring in one further note of qualification to my initial proposition, though this – by contrast with the first – is purely nominal. We can, if we so choose, extend the definition of class situation to embrace people's actual responses, in particular conjunctures of time, place and circumstance, to their locations in the web of inequality – their responses, too, to the parts they play in the chain of economic processes, in so far as economic role is separately relevant by the test I have suggested. In other words we can, if we like, include under the heading of class situation the whole range of questions which concern the extent to which people in this or that structurally defined class location recognise the inherent interests which, by sheer virtue of their place, they have in common with others in the same location; the forms and directions which such recognition takes; the economic relationships and other factors which help to shape, and at times to change, their responses in these senses. But it is a matter of semantics only whether we choose or decline to extend the definition of class situation in this way. Whichever we do, location in the complex of inequality (and in the complex of economic processes, where separately relevant) must come first in the sequence of analysis. The reason is simple: it makes little sense to consider how and why people respond, before we are clear what there is for them to respond to.

I need say little about my second proposition, because it follows directly from the first. It is that Marxist analysis of class in a capitalist mode of production – and, I am tempted to add, of capitalism itself – must keep constantly and firmly within its field of vision the principles and patterns of inequality distinctive of capitalism: its prescriptions for sub- and superordination; its characteristic mode of exploitation and the human impact of that, as much as the forms of control and subjection to control which distinguish it; the contours of privilege and deprivation as shaped by capitalism. Of course this does not mean that there is, or should be, no more to Marxist analysis of capitalism as a set of class relations and class situations than analysis of capitalist configurations of inequality: only that inequality must be kept clearly in sight, as a point for recurrent return, a signpost for repeated reference, wherever the analysis goes. To my own mind it also follows from these propositions, closely linked as they are, that Marxist social critique must in the end stand or fall by its capacity to set up, against its characterisation of capitalism, a viable conception of an alternative society free both from those forms and features of inequality distinctive of the capitalist order and from endemic inequality in any other significant manifestation. But that is not a point which I shall have time to follow through, more than obliquely at most, on this occasion.

These might once have seemed very obvious propositions. But if they were main presuppositions of Marxist inquiry twenty years ago, fifty years ago, indeed a hundred years ago, they have not been so – or very evidently so – more recently: in the balance and mood of Marxist research and debate over the last five, perhaps ten years. I at least have found myself quite often both puzzled and disturbed by contemporary western Marxist work in which the concrete differential impact of capitalist economic processes on people's lives and prospects – the distributional impact of capitalism, when 'distribution' is comprehensively conceived – seems to recede into remote distance: either to be neglected, though it may simultaneously be taken for granted; or to be brought into the picture only in a context of abstractions which, untranslated, leave the reality of human experience difficult to recognise.

To illustrate briefly, I might some little way back in time have pointed to characterisations of contemporary capitalism which, while placing 'alienation' at the centre of their concern, formulated their conceptions of the condition so elusively as virtually to preclude its concrete identification. More recent cases of what I have in mind include, for example, analyses of class structure that have brought to bear on the business of locating class boundaries a distinction between 'productive' and 'non-productive' labour which, whatever its validity for examination of economic processes, at best only partially and fortuitously corresponds to the distinctions created by the impact of inequality in the economic order of capitalism.[1] I see other, and theoretically quite closely related, examples in contributions to the critically important debate about the character of the state in western economies today which neglect to apply, in empirically supported detail, the test to their interpretations of the question 'who benefits?'; or again in the no more than tangential way in which controversies over the trend of profit have touched on the puzzles and implications of an apparent coexistence of evidence indicating a sustained fall in profits – profit shares as well as rates, by some measures – for a period now of up to two decades, with evidence suggesting little, except perhaps very recent, concomitant change in the general configuration of income inequality.[2] Symptomatic too, I think, has been an apparent reluctance of Marxists – some exceptions apart – to dig deep into the workings of public welfare provision, so that the running in this field and in associated exploration of 'poverty', by way of conceptual formulation no less than of empirical enquiry, has been left largely to others.

I do not, however, want to follow my initial propositions into the thickets of these examples, though one of the issues involved in several of them is central to this paper: that concerning the role of the state in contemporary western economies. I propose to take up one particular current interpretation of state activity which comes from outside, not from within, the Marxist fold; and to suggest that, in the answers which in my view Marxist analysis must make to this interpretation, examination of the mode of exploitation characteristic of capitalism needs to figure centrally. My focus will be less on this interpretation in itself – one version of several contemporary characterisations of the state as 'corporatist' – than on the opportunity it offers, and I would argue the obligation it imposes, for Marxists to work through their own conceptions of the capitalist order today. With that as my focus and in illustration of my initial propositions, I hope to convince you of the crucial part which diagnosis of the principles and patterns of prevalent inequality has to play in any Marxist responses to the challenge posed by the central postulate of the interpretation in question. This is a postulate that changes in the character of state activity now point to the replacement of capitalism by a distinct economic order: a 'corporatist' order which is neither capitalist nor socialist, but which exists in its own right as a distinct social system or mode of production.

My choice could provoke an objection that there is little pay-off for Marxist analysis in digging away at 'bourgeois' analysis. I would disagree. Leave aside whether the 'corporatist' thesis in the version I have in mind has so little anchorage in Marxist thought that the label 'bourgeois' fits at all neatly: a moot point, but not one which I want to labour. The larger risk that goes with this kind of objection is to accentuate an intellectual and political isolation of Marxism. Paradoxically, the revival and diversification of western Marxist thought in the last couple of decades have, in some ways, also made for more of such isolation. When self-confessed Marxists were very few and far between, they could hold back from the business of grappling with opposing social interpretations only at the evident price of becoming an esoteric cult. The sheer arithmetic of larger numbers and greater diversity has now made it easier, and more tempting, for Marxists to keep securely within their own universe of discourse. But when they do so, they blunt both their intellectual cutting edge and their political impact. There is no divide so absolute between Marxist and all other social interpretation (academic or lay), no lack of common ground in premises of thought so total, that Marxism has nothing to gain from any mode of approach outside its own fold; that acceptance or rejection of Marxism in the end rests only on an arbitrary choice between rival and irreconcilable axioms; that Marxist constructions of social reality can gain (or lose) adherents only by conversion to (or from) the presuppositions of Marxism, not by weight of argument and evidence in confrontation with contrary constructions. Marxism is not a theology, valid only within its own terms and for those who accept its terms. Its advance, intellectually no less than politically, now as before, must come in considerable part from engagement with influential or persuasive alternative theory.

II

The theory of 'creeping corporatisation' which I shall take as my object lesson certainly shows signs of gaining influence in public and academic debate; and there are persuasive features to it. 'Corporatism', of course, is a tag which has frequently been tied in recent years to developments in western economic and political organisation; but with a bewildering variety of meanings, embedded in very diverse interpretations of the larger context of these developments and their implications, carrying references of different kinds – or none of note – to corporatism in Fascist Italy and Nazi Germany. One well publicised version, however, stands out both for its lucidity and sophistication in elaboration; and, above all, for its distinct and explicit assertion that the corporatist order on whose brink we are said to stand – in which Britain, most likely, will be fully immersed by the 1980s – constitutes an economic system of a kind by itself, qualitatively different from both capitalism and socialism. This is the version argued by Jack Winkler, in collaboration and occasional co-authorship with Ray Pahl.[3] Stripped to its barest bones, the thesis can be summarised in three points.

First, a process has been going on in Britain among other western countries since the 1960s which, if sustained as is probable, will soon bring to culmination a fundamental change in the relationship between state and private business. The state has acquired, is acquiring, and can be expected to extend its acquisition of, effective powers of control over business policy which go well beyond those powers of support, guidance and differential intervention which were associated with earlier phases in the growth of state activity. These powers include, crucially, control – *de jure* in some ways, *de facto* still more – over profits, prices and investment as well as wages and salaries: control, in short, over the key variables hitherto subject to determination by business policy and market forces; control capable of direction, and in fact directed at will, to individual businesses and particular sectors of the economy, not merely to setting or modifying an overall climate in which decisions are still made and their criteria determined by private enterprise; control much further reaching than that involved either in policies of wage restraint by themselves or in combinations of forecasting, persuasion, publicity and occasional special aid designed to coordinate investment still undertaken on fragmented initiative.

Legal ownership of business stays predominantly in private hands, however, although its substance is much diminished. The privileges of property no longer include the right and effective capacity to take those crucial decisions about resource allocation formerly regarded as prerogatives of private ownership. Even the right to extract profit is hedged with restrictions. But state appropriation of these powers of control and constraint has left, and will continue to leave, an elaborate façade of private property in being; and by the same token managerial responsibility for the implementation of state-determined policy, managerial authority over labour, remain in largest part matters for private enterprise. It is that conjunction of state control with private legal ownership and private exercise of everyday management which, so the argument goes, in the first instance signals the emergence of a new corporatist economic system. The qualitative range of state control marks it off from capitalism. The retention of the legal framework and managerial machinery of private property – coupled with the guidance of state policy by an assumption that 'distinct class and functional interests' must remain but 'must be made to collaborate'[4] – marks it off from socialism.

Second, according to this thesis, state control in its new and far-reaching forms is steered by four principles. It is these guiding ideas which together give corporatist policy its distinctive stamp. One is *unity*, a sanctification of cooperation in place of competition as the means of economic salvation. Another is *order*, the application of discipline and collective self-restraint to economic affairs in place of both market anarchy and industrial conflict. The third is *nationalism*:

prosperity is sought for the nation considered as an entity, over and against the particular interests of particular groups or the freedom of individuals to make their own ways to success or failure; and in mercantilist assertion of a common national interest vis-à-vis other nations and economic operations controlled from abroad. The fourth guiding principle on the list is *success*, a commitment to results with scant concern for means: corporatist policy, in this characterisation, is prepared to ride roughshod over the rule of law to realise its objectives.

The principle of 'success' – the priority said to be accorded to efficacy over maintenance of legal rights and liberal-democratic safeguards – looms sufficiently large to merit elaboration as the third main element in Winkler's picture of the emerging corporatist system. State control, extensive though it is, is exercised in large measure indirectly; behind the scenes rather than openly; by discretionary use of financial force, bargaining strength and elastically defined authority, in ways which shield decision-making in economic affairs from effective public scrutiny. In so far as legislation is needed, the model preferred is that of the enabling act, which confers large and loosely bounded administrative powers on government and its agents. The illustrative prototype, in Winkler's presentation, is the Industry Act 1975, a Labour Government measure; the prototypical means of state economic direction is the series of 'planning agreements' between government and private business corporations which it was a purpose of that Act to promote. The crucial decisions on resource allocation will be made in negotiations between state and private enterprise; but with the state, so the argument runs, in a position generally to ensure business compliance in its policy and in the principles of 'unity', 'order', 'nationalism' and 'success' to which that policy is geared. Delegation is the order of the day. Parliament delegates policy-making to government; government delegates policy-implementation and managerial authority to business; trade unions, too, are recruited as agents for the execution of government policy – to enforce wage restraint and labour discipline – in so far as they can be reliably co-opted. But the power to shape policy, to prevail in the processes of bargaining in Whitehall, corporation and union offices where investment, expansion and contraction are determined, prices, profits and wage-levels set – that power is with the state.

III

There are, of course, significant touches to this diagnosis reminiscent of much earlier commentary on the course and prospects of western industrial societies. Both the growth of state activity and a progressive separation of control from ownership are familiar threads in familiar arguments that capitalism is in process of erosion, if it is not already fully eroded. But the valuation which goes with this version of an old theme is hostile. There is nothing to it of the complacency characteristic of those brands of the thesis of 'managerial infiltration' current in the 1950s and 1960s, which attributed a benign and civilising effect to postulated managerial supremacy; or of the parallel complacency characteristic of conventional interpretations of state activity in a 'mixed economy' as directed to curbing capitalist excess and promoting popular welfare. The tone of Winkler's commentary, restrained though it is, has far more echoes of Burnham's assessment of managerial revolution and of those contemporary prophecies of doom – laissez-faire right and liberal-radical left alike – which have pointed to bureaucratic usurpation of power as the prime present and prospective source of human oppression. Winkler's version is gloomy. Corporatism, as he sees it, involves a removal of policy-making from exposure to public scrutiny. If the economic decisions of private enterprise before the corporatist phase were hard enough to challenge, because they were private, the state's decisions today and tomorrow are no less concealed, no less effectively irresponsible; and the concentration of power in state hands is the more dangerous because it is insidious. While corporatism – most probably in Britain, at least – will continue to leave the formal shells of liberal democracy and legal procedure intact, it embeds the real exercise of power in processes of policy determination which will rarely and only fragmentarily be visible at large.

This emphasis on a simultaneous proliferation and screening of places where decisions are made is not, however, central to the logic of Winkler's argument that corporatism constitutes an economic system qualitatively distinct from capitalism. Reliance on administrative discretion, on delegation, on bargaining and pressure applied offstage in a multitude of mediating bodies and settings where government, business and unions meet – this is all characteristic of current trends in the organisation of economy and polity, and well described by Winkler. But the validity of that description gives no answer to the question whether the state is still tail, wagged by a business dog; or has become dog itself, wagging a business tail: whether, in short, corporatism operates within capitalism or must be seen as a mode of production *sui generis*. Nor does Winkler pin his designation of corporatism as a separate order to his description of the machinery of decision-making currently emerging in Britain. It is not the balance between direct and indirect forms of state control, between dictation and persuasion, between repression and cooptation, which is central; that may vary over time and from one corporatist order to another. The keystone of his argument is the postulated fact of state direction, whatever its forms, and its conjunction with a continuing framework of private property and private managerial authority. Corporatism, in his own summary phase, is 'an economic system of private ownership and state control'.[5]

It should be obvious that this reading of a funeral sermon over capitalism cannot be dismissed merely by a counter-assertion that capitalism remains so long as private ownership remains. That would be to retreat into semantics: to adopt a tactic of evasion by means of definition which Winkler, quite reasonably, forestalls when he says that his concern is not with labels. It is with the reality of processes which, whatever names may best describe them, point in his eyes to a fragmentation of property rights whereby their major substance passes into state hands. Nor is it sufficient in rebuttal – though it is relevant – to pick out features in the ideology schematically attributed to corporatist policy which have a long history in the corpus of dominant ideas associated with an uncontestably capitalist economic system. Conservative, if not laissez-faire liberal, appeals for 'order' – the moral elevation of social discipline over individual and group self-interest, of social harmony as a natural condition with dissent as an aberration triggered by myopia – have been a perennial refrain in education and exhortation directed especially at labour. Successful capitalist enterprise has long sought – and invoked state aid – to consolidate its success by eliminating the insecurity engendered by market competition: 'unity' in that sense is no new aspiration. 'Nationalist' protection of domestic private enterprise has been the rule rather than the exception in capitalist economies. Yet the presence of well-worn elements in the guiding principles of corporatist policy – cursorily though Winkler recognises their familiarity, when he does so at all – is not enough to make the case against him. For these elements, so the logic of the argument appears to be, acquire new force and new significance when they come together as the bearing ideas in a new context. It is the shift of context which is the issue: the postulated subordination of economic decisions on key matters to state direction.

So any critique must focus on just that contention; and it must test it, I suggest, by asking three closely related questions. First, in what sense, if at all sensibly, can the state be said to direct: where in fact are the sources of control over economic affairs? Next, whatever the sources of control, what are the criteria by which it is exercised: what yardsticks and operating assumptions are used to allocate resources? What finally – and I shall suggest that this is the decisive question, the answer to which will subsume the answers to the other two – is the distributional outcome: to whose benefit, by what principles of interest and justice?

IV

These, in my view, are the issues central to any characterisation of an economic system, any attempt to demarcate one mode of production from others. Winkler's analysis, however, is addressed in the main only to the first question. The other two receive short shrift. Even in his answers to the first, moreover, there are noticeable gaps.

One gap concerns the conception of the state. Concede, if only for the sake of argument, that the state has aquired the decisive means of economic control attributed to it; and certainly recent British governments have taken a series of powers over prices and profits as well as labour earnings which, joined to government disposal over large funds for selective deployment in industry, lend initial credibility to the thesis. The question then looms large: what is the nature of this state, ostensibly capable of directing privately owned business this way or that? There is no clear answer; hardly even the outlines of one. True, in an appendix note Winkler recognises the question, and translates it from the form 'what is the state?' to the form 'what does the state do?'[6] The translation is reasonable enough; and it might well be elaborated.

To ask what the state is must be, in large part, to ask what the state does; but to ask what it does must be, in equally large part, to ask what concrete interests the state serves, supports or aids by its actions. In fact, translated or untranslated, the question is left to hang in the air. The existence of state powers of control does not by itself tell us how they are, or will be, used. The four guiding principles of state policy, as I shall argue later, do not by themselves identify particular objectives or criteria of resource allocation. With both ends and actions unspecified, the interests to which state policy in effect is directed remain equally indefinite. The state, for all the powers attributed to it, floats in a vacuum, a paradoxically unknown quantity.

There are points at which Winkler suggests – or the argument in all logic implies – that state policy is shaped by a variety of 'outside' pressures: popular pressures, for example, to trim monopoly profits. But the nature and direction of such influences upon state policy, above all their relative impact on the outcome if and when they pull different ways, are issues left unexplored and barely even identified. In turn, that neglect of the balance among prevailing winds suggests an alternative assumption that there are no prevailing winds which matter very much. *Either*, then, the state is in some absolute sense an autonomous entity: a creature with will and interest of its own – of some or all of its office holders in this or that combination of influence – to infuse into state use of the means of economic control. But if that is the assumption, this 'state will' *sui generis* – the directing 'collective conscience' of a corporatist system which merits designation as an economic order *sui generis* – remains unexplained. Its sources, formation and direction are not described. *Or* perhaps, as some passages imply, 'state will' cannot effectively be distinguished from the 'wills' of significant 'outside' interests, because state policy objectives in a corporatist context largely coincide with the policy objectives accepted by other interests: interests co-opted, cajoled, pressed into service as agents of the state. But that formulation is no better designed to close the gap in analysis. For if the state is assigned a dominant role, its 'dominance' must mean that there is at least a logical divergence between its interests and those of other significant bodies and groups: at least an initial, maybe a perenially latent, divergence of interests, though this in practice is resolved or suppressed by the state's postulated capacity to bring about 'outside' endorsement of its policy objectives. So in this version too the state appears to be an entity in its own right: separate not just as a collection of institutions and people who man them, but as a cluster of initially and conceptually distinct interests. And the point stands that this conception is left, not only unspecified, but hardly even noted as a matter for specification.

If the state thus, whichever way one takes it, figures in a curiously disembodied form, so also its ability to put the powers which it has acquired to uses of its own is only asserted, not demonstrated. That ability, so the argument implies, will be tested and found true largely in processes of negotiation and manipulation behind the scenes, when representatives of government, business, unions and sometimes other groups meet to settle the terms of production and exchange. If a 'pluralist' methodological prescription were adopted to assess the hypothesis that the state will prevail in such bargaining, these processes themselves would need systematic observation. The 'inputs' from the various contending parties would have to be compared with the outcome, to establish the locus – or possibly shifting loci – of power. Winkler does not attempt to clinch his case in this manner; nor does he suggest that the hypothesis remains untested until such research is undertaken. A pluralist procedure would in any case be insufficient for the purpose, as for all attempts to identify power, because it would leave out of consideration the ways in which areas for reciprocal bargaining and pressure are predetermined by prior assumptions on the part of the contending parties about the limits of their potential influence and the bounds of practicable policy 'in the world as it is'. Such predetermination of the contestable, with its implicit acceptance of continuity in all matters not defined as contestable, reflects the larger context of power within which particular juggling for influence takes place.[7] Winkler indeed suggests just some such prior confinement of areas of dispute to a narrow range, when he refers to business and union endorsement of objectives which he ascribes to government. But he neither shows, nor sets out criteria by which to show, the validity of his interpretation that this concordance marks a practical and ideological predominance of state over business and unions – rather than, say, of business over state and unions. Yet that, after all, is just the point at issue.

V

To tackle it one must look at the purpose and substance of the measures of state direction which are said to define corporatism. More particularly, one must look at the criteria for resource allocation which appear to govern such economic decisions as government takes with the powers it has, or as government underwrites when relevant decisions seem to be taken by private business and others whom Winkler casts in the role of state agents. In short, an answer to the first of the three test questions which I outlined earlier, the question concerning sources of control, requires an answer to the second: by what yardsticks and operational assumptions are key economic decisions made? For the hypothesis to stand up that corporatism is a mode of production *sui generis*, categorically distinct from capitalism, these yardsticks and assumptions must be correspondingly distinct from those which determine resource allocation in a capitalist system.

There is little in Winkler's analysis, however, and still less in the real world as it appears to me, to confirm that there are such new and distinct economic criteria at work. The four guiding 'principles' of corporatist policy set no prescriptions for allocation of resources. They are empty vessels into which this, that or another formula for investment and production may be poured. The formula could well be that characteristic of capitalism, under which resources are allocated in general to achieve long-run profit maximisation: corporatist concerns for 'unity' and 'order', 'nation' and 'success' need in no significant way clash with the general use of profit yardsticks. Market competition may in all likelihood indeed be progressively curtailed and the need for 'unity' invoked in justification. But the ascendance of oligopoly and monopoly, as Winkler recognises for other purposes of his argument, is a familiar trend within capitalism; and it does not by itself signify any displacement of profit optimisation from its role in economic decisions. Injunctions for 'order' – especially when directed to labour to hold wage claims back and discourage industrial unrest, but in other forms too – similarly carry no definite prescriptions for resource allocation alternative to the profit criterion. 'Nationalist' policies of protection against foreign economic penetration – including protection against multinational corporations whose main weight is abroad – may or may not be perverse according to classical doctrine. But they make as good sense to threatened domestic business enterprise, concerned to secure and enhance its own profitability, as does state-supported restraint of domestic market competition to those firms who are thereby enabled to mark up safer and larger returns to their capital. Corporatist policy may very well put 'success' before adherence to liberal-democratic conceptions of due legal process and parliamentary scrutiny. But that neither says how economic success is measured, nor points to a substitution of new modes of measurement for the old mode of reference to profit.

So far, I have put my argument on this score cautiously, in a verbally agnostic form. The four principles of corporatist policy are instrumental in character: they prescribe means of approach to economic ends, but not ends themselves. They are elastic: capable of accommodating objectives of long-run business profitability no less than possible alternatives.[8] The inference is obvious: if no alternative objectives can be read off from these principles, what is there then to support an assumption that some alternative is, nevertheless, in operation? But the point can be put more positively. Quite sweeping in compass though they may seem, government controls in the 1960s and 1970s have had one overriding purpose: to restore profitability to private business in face of a persistent trend of falling profits. There is no equivalence of weight among the various measures adopted. Wage restraint in diverse forms has been a pre-eminent and constant element in the armoury of government regulation. Selective encouragement of investment and production – so far to little avail – has been another recurrent feature. Price codes and other forms of potential restraint on profits, by contrast, have figured less; in weaker and more nominal forms – as exercises in public relations, especially, to evoke popular and trade union support for wage restraint; and quite explicitly as temporary devices, for a long-run rehabilitation of profit. It would take a comprehensive review of government measures, government statements of purpose, government policy in its outcome, to establish this beyond all shadow of doubt. That is not possible here. But even cursory reflection on the history of state intervention over the last decade or two points to the plausibility of this reading far more than of the converse construction that some alternative – and unspecified – set of objectives has replaced profit optimisation as the measure of economic success and the prime criterion for allocation of resources.

Winkler acknowledges the crisis of falling profits as one main cause of emergent corporatism. But he neither, of course, pursues the point into an interpretation of corporatist state activity as a strategy to restore profitability and so to maintain the *modus operandi* of a capitalist order. Nor does he dispose of that possibility by argument to the contrary. In another factor identified as a mainspring of corporatisation, however, he sees a source of direct state opposition to the working principles of capitalism. Here is the one point at which he specifically postulates an erosion of profit optimisation as the criterion of resource allocation, instead of merely leaving his readers to infer such erosion from the growth of state economic activity. The steady trend of industrial concentration, so this part of the argument runs, produces business monopolies whose unrestrained consequences it is impossible for governments to tolerate. Private ownership must be generally maintained: the corporate state is a reluctant nationaliser. But if private ownership is to stay, the excess profits of monpoly privilege must be curtailed. Neither government nor business can retain their legitimacy unless monopoly profits are trimmed.

The argument looks lame. Occasional and partial state action to cut back monpoly profits in one or other particular instance no more sets aside pursuit of profit as the prime motor of economic enterprise than does the existence of government machinery to investigate, and occasionally to obstruct, the continuous processes of industrial concentration from which monopolies arise.[9] Business interests are not uniform on this matter: they are neither consistently for nor consistently against monopoly. In any given set of circumstances, restrictions on competition which strengthen one firm or sector are likely to harm others. No intention or effect hostile to the capitalist order can be read into any form of state intervention against monopoly formation or monopoly profit – conversely, for that matter, any form of monopoly promotion by the state – unless it is so sustained and directed as to make the principle of profit optimisation inoperable. It is hard to see the signs of such a reversal of the wheel of profit in spasmodic and limited government forays into this or that odd corner of 'excess' profit; let alone to see signs of that sort in the rhetoric of government exercises in public relations which concede the existence of an 'unacceptable face' to capitalism while failing to delineate the specific features of that face and, therefore, of necessity, to specify measures – logically called for by the phrase – to remove what is 'unacceptable' and leave what is 'acceptable'.

Take the issue a little further, however. Imagine that state activity were in fact directed in a regular and consistent manner against monopoly profit; and to a point where profitability could no longer serve as the normal criterion of resource allocation. That, clearly, would signify some such dethronement of private capital from the centre of decision making as Winkler has in mind. But the consequence of this imaginary experiment is, once more, to expose the gap in his analysis on the question of sources of control. For whence would the effective impetus for such policy on the part of the state have come? Not from business, evidently enough, even if business were eventually persuaded to accept the outcome. Instead, it is implied, from popular opinion pressing successfully upon government the view that monopoly profits cannot be tolerated. If so, however, the mechanics by which such pressure takes effect is obscure. 'Popular' pressures must here mean, in practice, pressures which are channelled largely into and through the labour movement: at work, presumably, in and behind elections and especially in those processes of bargaining off-stage where representatives of unions, government and business meet to thrash out the terms of economic conduct. Government ascendancy – the defining characteristic of corporatism, so we are told – must then, in respect of the key issue whether profit should retain or lose its role in resource allocation, imply at least partial labour and union ascendancy. Yet that logical inference is not set out, let alone pursued in any attempt to describe the balance among the forces which may bear upon the making of corporatist policies. Nor is the inference easy to reconcile with current political and industrial realities in Britain, the effectively predominant elements in whose labour movement have so far shown more practical concern to run capitalism with greater efficiency – and some pay-off for labour – than to subvert capitalism by rendering the principle of private profit inoperable. Whether labour organisations *might* attempt to use the machinery of state intervention to subvert the capitalist economic order is one thing. Whether they actually do so – and then, to boot, succeed – is quite another, of which no evidence is offered.

VI

Still, fragile though the hypothesis is on all these scores, let me imagine once more that it were in fact true, in order to follow the logic of the argument wherever it may then lead. For corporatism to have displaced capitalism, so I have suggested, the latter's mode of productive resource allocation by reference to long-run profit maximisation must have been displaced by some alternative mode. But by what? It is at this point that the last of the three test questions which I listed earlier comes into play: to whose benefit? For if state policy determines production and investment by criteria other than profitability, those alternative criteria must reflect some conception of 'public interest', of the 'national good', of societal benefit; and that conception must rest on stated or unstated principles of justice – principles of 'distributive allocation' – distinct from those which characterise capitalism and follow from the role accorded to private profit in the economic machinery of capitalism.

In fact, no such distinctive ethic of distribution appears to mark off corporatism from capitalism in this characterisation. One of the four postulated principles of policy might, at first sight, suggest the makings of an alternative philosophy of resource allocation for production and consumption alike: one could perhaps read into the concern with 'nation' and 'national' achievement a concern with economic growth at large, 'for its own sake'. But there is no key to the criteria of economic decisions to be found there. If growth *per se* were the prime objective of policy – just to play along with that assumption – alternatives between growth in this sector and in that, between investment in one line of production and in another, would still have to be weighed in the balance. The yardstick by which such choices are made in a capitalist economy is that of long-run profit. If it were no longer profit, it could only be some conception of 'general good' – which might, of course, neatly coincide with the good of those who made policy; and any such conception would have to include answers to the question 'who is to benefit, more and less, most and least?'. Without answers to that question – answers quite possibly taken for granted, assumed rather than openly asserted – no allocation of resources among alternative uses could take place. Distributional principles, in short, are necessarily involved in allocation for production and investment. In a capitalist order, as I shall go on to argue in conclusion, the principles which prevail follow inextricably from the profit criterion and the institutions of private property and markets which are its operational context. In any state- or publicly-directed order to which capitalism might give way, such principles would be an inescapable, even if perhaps inexplicit, ingredient of policy.

It seems, however, that corporatist principles of distribution in Winkler's model merely echo those at work in the capitalist system which corporatism is supposed to be replacing. The point is not just — though it is important — that the prerogatives of everyday managerial authority remain with private capital. It is also that the pattern of economic privilege and deprivation — hence in addition, one must assume, all or most of what goes with that by way of inequalities in opportunity and culture — remains in all essence as within a capitalist order. Corporatism, of course, is and will be inegalitarian in social thrust. It harbours, as Winkler underlines, 'no principle favouring redistribution or equality . . . corporatism is in principle hierarchical.'[10] Power and authority are, by imperative of corporatist morality, to be unequally distributed. Material rewards might not be, by reference to principle alone. But, he continues, they are almost bound, of sociological necessity, to follow the hierarchical pattern of power and authority. The mere presence of marked inequality, however, does not make my case for me. Capitalism is not defined by the fact that inequality is inherent in its social being. If it were, all complex societies in history hitherto would merit designation as 'capitalist': that way lies analytical bankruptcy. What does make my case is, neither the existence nor even the sheer quantity of inequality within 'corporatism', but its quality: the sources of privilege and deprivation, the principles which govern their allocation. For these, it seems clear, are the same sources and the same principles by which class inequality is set within capitalism. Certainly no others are identified; and no others, I suggest, can be seen on the horizon.

I need to be explicit. Contemporary capitalist rules of distributional justice in the sphere of consumption are largely unstated; but they are clear enough. There are three main principles. The *first* is that property ownership constitutes, of itself, a claim on resources for livelihood provided, for full effect, that owners put their assets into the market to yield income. Two corollaries follow. Because ownership or productive resources is highly concentrated, it makes a large contribution to overall inequality in the means of life. It also for the same reason confers effective immunity on a privileged minority from the ethic of work to which all others are subject. The *second* principle is that people without substantial property must, to obtain more than a minimal livelihood, hire out their labour power in markets geared to produce optimum long-run returns to property; or they must depend on others — members of their own households — who so hire out their labour power. Two corollaries follow again. The propertyless hire out their labour power in diverse markets, on quite widely different terms; and a relatively few — members of well-established professions, for example — do so in markets over which they themselves have considerable collective control. From this comes a proliferation of economic gradations, and of vested interests and inter-grade conflicts, which in part obscure the larger pattern of principled inequity. What is involved, moreover, is an institutionalisation of monetary incentives which both erects barriers to redistribution by reform and, through its concrete buttressing of an ethic of work, makes a fertile soil for popular animus against 'scrounging'. The *third* principle follows directly. People who have neither property nor a means of livelihood from hiring out of labour power must and can now rely — with varying degrees of security in different capitalist economies of the contemporary West — on state support in cash and kind. But state support is set in principle, in order to maintain monetary incentives and in consonance with the ethic of work, at levels generally below those of appropriately corresponding labour market earnings. So, among other consequences, the proliferation of economic gradations is extended further; and the 'poor' are made to appear in a separate set of categories from the wage-earning majority of the propertyless. The logic of the three principles, and their essential interconnections as a single system of rules of distributive justice, is thereby once again veiled.

VII

Nothing in the characterisation of corporatism against which I have argued suggests that these principles are, or will be, significantly changed by the postulated transition from capitalism. By that test of substance, as by the others which I have advanced, the change in nomenclature of the economic system fails again. But the purpose of my argument is not just to drive home that conclusion; or even mainly that, although I have spent much time on it. It is also and more centrally to make the point, by this illustration, that capitalism as an economic order must be defined by reference to its mode of distribution – its mode of exploitation – no less than by reference to its mode of productive organisation. These modes, indeed, cannot be separated. 'Production' does not hang in the air, unrelated to the markets in which produce is sold; in which labour power as well as raw materials are exchanged; through which surplus is extracted from labour. The three test questions which I have applied to the hypothesis that corporatism is an economic system hang together; and they do so in a significant sequence. From the question about sources of control, because the locus of power cannot be established only by simple observation of decision-making behaviour, we are led to ask about the criteria of resource allocation which guide control over production and investment. From that question in turn, because criteria for resource allocation for production and investment inescapably imply criteria of distribution, we are led to ask about the principles of social justice which, express or implicit, inform allocation for life and livelihood. Class inequality, in short, has a distinctive quality in capitalism, which is central to the identification of capitalism as an economic order.

REFERENCES

1. See especially N. Poulantzas, *Classes in Contemporary Capitalism*, New Left Books, 1975; and for a cogent criticism, E. O. Wright, 'Class boundaries in advanced capitalist societies', *New Left Review*, 98, July/Aug. 1976.
2. Cf. J. H. Westergaard and H. Resler, *Class in a Capitalist Society*, Heinemann, 1975, Penguin Books, 1976; and Royal Commission on the Distribution of Income and Wealth, report no. 1, *Initial Report on the Standing Reference* (Cmnd 6171) HMSO, 1975. The Royal Commission's report no. 4, *Second Report on the Standing Reference* (Cmnd 6626) suggests some narrowing of inequality between 1972–73 and 1973–74. But this would be significant only if sustained. Moreover, the post-tax gains indicated on the part of the poorest 20 per cent came at the expense of the next 30 per cent above them and of the decile group 11–20 per cent (at the expense, generally, of wage- and low-to-middle-grade salary earners); not of the wealthiest 10 per cent, or indeed of the top 1 per cent. Finally, both the 1972/3–1973/4 shift, and such signs as are pointed to in the Royal Commission reports of slight longer-term reductions in income inequality at the extremes of the scale, are open to question on points concerning the allowances needed for

unrecorded real income and for possible changes in the ratio of such income to recorded income, especially among the wealthiest. On the 'profits squeeze', see in particular A. Glyn and B. Sutcliffe, *British Capitalism, Workers and the Profits Squeeze*, Penguin Books, 1972; A. Glyn 'Notes on the profits squeeze', *Bull. Conference Socialist Economists*, Feb. 1975; and for further references, mainly to theoretical discussion about the trend of profit, B. Fine and L. Harris, 'Controversial issues in Marxist economic theory', *Socialist Register 1976*. It is worth pointing out that data indicating a concomitant decline in the shares of total product going to *both* employment income and profits would indicate a real shift in distribution only if the third and growing share by this form of measurement — that of the state — were of disproportionate benefit to labour: an empirically dubious proposition.

3. J. T. Winkler, 'Law, state and economy: the Industry Act 1975 in context', *British J. Law and Society*, Winter 1975; *idem*, 'Corporatism', *European J. Sociology*, vol. 17, no. 1, 1976. Articles on the same subject by Winkler and R. E. Pahl have also appeared in *The Times* and *New Society*.

4. Winkler, loc. cit. 1976, p. 106.

5. Winkler, loc, cit. 1976, p. 109.

6. Winkler, loc. cit. 1976, pp. 134–6.

7. Cf. Westergaard and Resler, op. cit., part III, chapters 1 and 7; see also S. Lukes, *Power: a radical view*, Macmillan, 1974.

8. Much the same point can be made in criticism of an argument that nationalisation of industry in Britain has represented a partial ascendancy of 'professionalism', as a prescription for economic management, over the ethic and operating principles of capitalist business enterprise (M. Burrage, 'Nationalization and the professional ideal', *Sociology*, May 1973). 'Professionalism' may prescribe 'public service', but it does not by itself define the criteria and objectives of 'public service'.

9. Winkler (e.g., loc. cit. 1976, pp. 132–3) toys briefly with an alternative scenario for the next few years, in which the trend would be a return towards capitalism through state anti-monopoly policies (and removal of protection against foreign competition), designed 'to restore a competitive market economy'. He clearly sees such measures as quite different in implication from measures to clip the profits of monopolies otherwise tolerated. But his apparent identification here, and in some other places, of capitalism with economic competition is difficult to accept and to reconcile with the general line of his argument that corporatism, as a new economic order, is distinguished by a combination of state control with private ownership; not by diminution of market competition which, whether aided or obstructed by the state, is a well-established trend, long preceding the postulated arrival of corporatism.

10. Winkler, loc. cit. 1976, p. 107.

NOTES ON CONTRIBUTORS

Stuart Hall is Director of the Centre for Contemporary Cultural Studies at Birmingham University. He has written widely on the media and youth culture including (with Tony Jefferson) *Resistance Through Rituals* (Hutchinson, 1976), as well as 'Marx's Notes on Method', in *Working Papers in Cultural Studies*, no. 6 (1974) and 'Re-thinking the "Base-and-Superstructure" Metaphor', in *Class, Hegemony and Party* (ed. Jon Bloomfield, Lawrence and Wishart, 1977).

Vic Allen is Professor of the Sociology of Industrial Society at the University of Leeds. He is the author of several books on trade unionism, including *Militant Trade Unionism* (Merlin, 1966), *Sociology of Industrial Relations* (Longmans, 1971); and also *Social Analysis: A Marxist Critique and Alternative* (Longman, 1975).

Alan Hunt is the Secretary of the Sociology Group of the Communist Party, and is Assistant-Dean at Middlesex Polytechnic. He is author of a number of articles, including 'Class Structure in Britain Today' in *Marxism Today* (June, 1970), 'Law, State and Class Struggle' in *Marxism Today* (June, 1976), and 'Lenin and Sociology' in *Sociological Review* (February, 1976).

Nicos Poulantzas is a member of the Greek Communist Party (Interior) and lectures in the department of sociology at the University of Vincennes. His books in English translation are *Political Power and Social Classes* (1973), *Fascism and Dictatorship* (1974), *Classes in Contemporary Capitalism* (1975) and *The Crisis of the Dictatorships* (1976); all are published by New Left Books.

Paul Hirst is a Lecturer in Sociology at Birkbeck College, University of London. He is the author of *Durkheim, Bernard and Epistemology* (Routledge and Kegan Paul, 1975), *Social Evolution and Sociological Categories* (Allen and Unwin, 1976); and, with Barry Hindess, of *Pre-Capitalist Modes of Production* (Routledge and Kegan Paul, 1975), and *Mode of Production and Social Formation* (Macmillan, 1977).

Jean Gardiner is a lecturer in the Department of Adult Education and Extra-Mural Studies at the University of Leeds. She has been active in the Women's Liberation Movement since 1970, and is a member of the Communist Party. She has published 'Women's Domestic Labour' in *New Left Review*, 89 (1975), and *Women in Society*, Course Unit, Open University Press (1976).

John Westergaard is Professor of Sociological Studies at the University of Sheffield. He is the author (with Henrietta Resler) of *Class in a Capitalist Society* (Heinemann, 1975, and Penguin, 1976).

NAME INDEX

No entries are given for Marx or Engels as their names occur throughout the volume